Building a New Foundation for Innovation

Results of a Workshop for the National Science Foundation

T0154930

Eric V. Larson
Irene T. Brahmakulam

Prepared for the
National Science Foundation

Science and Technology Policy Institute

RAND

The research described in this report was conducted by RAND's Science and Technology Policy Institute for the National Science Foundation under Contract ENG-9812731.

Library of Congress Cataloging-in-Publication Data

Larson, Eric V. (Eric Victor), 1957–
   Building a new foundation for innovation : results of a workshop for the National Science Foundation / Eric V. Larson, Irene T. Brahmakulam.
      p. cm.
   "MR-1534."
   Includes bibliographical references.
   ISBN 0-8330-3158-9
   1. Partnerships for Innovation. 2. Research and development partnership—United States. 3. Academic-industrial collaboration—United States. I. Brahmakulam, Irene T. II. Title.

Q180.U5 L37 2001
338.97306—dc21

                                                                    2002024931

Published 2002 by RAND
1700 Main Street, P.O. Box 2138, Santa Monica, CA 90407-2138
1200 South Hayes Street, Arlington, VA 22202-5050
201 North Craig Street, Suite 102, Pittsburgh, PA 15213
RAND URL: http://www.rand.org/
To order RAND documents or to obtain additional information, contact Distribution Services: Telephone: (310) 451-7002; Fax: (310) 451-6915; Email: order@rand.org

This report summarizes the results of a National Science Foundation workshop, *Partnerships: Building a New Foundation for Innovation,* held June 18–19, 2001, in Arlington, Virginia. The workshop and this report were sponsored by the National Science Foundation's Partnerships for Innovation program and were conducted within RAND's Science and Technology Policy Institute.

ABOUT THE S&T POLICY INSTITUTE

Originally created by Congress in 1991 as the Critical Technologies Institute and renamed in 1998, the Science and Technology Policy Institute is a federally funded research and development center sponsored by the National Science Foundation and managed by RAND. The Institute's mission is to help improve public policy by conducting objective, independent research and analysis on policy issues that involve science and technology. To this end, the Institute

- Supports the Office of Science and Technology Policy and other Executive Branch agencies, offices, and councils;

- Helps science and technology decisionmakers understand the likely consequences of their decisions and choose among alternative policies; and

- Helps improve understanding in both the public and private sectors of the ways in which science and technology can better serve national objectives.

In carrying out its mission, the Institute consults broadly with representatives from private industry, institutions of higher education, and other nonprofit institutions.

Inquiries regarding the Science and Technology Policy Institute may be directed to the address below.

Helga E. Rippen
Director
Science and Technology Policy Institute
1200 South Hayes Street
Arlington, VA 22202
Phone: (703) 413-1100 ext. 5351
Email: stpi@rand.org

CONTENTS

Appendix

TABLES

- Broaden the participation of all types of academic institutions and all citizens in NSF activities to more fully meet the broad workforce needs of the national innovation enterprise; and

- Catalyze creation of the enabling infrastructure necessary to foster and sustain long-term innovation.

This report summarizes the results of discussions that took place during a 1-1/2 day workshop that convened in June 2001 to consider the PFI program and the NSF's role in the larger national innovation enterprise.[2] These discussions can be summarized broadly in terms of what was said about innovation and how best to measure it, about partnerships and how they might be assessed, and about what the National Science Foundation might do to foster innovation generally, and more specifically, through partnerships.

INNOVATION

Although the NSF as yet has not embraced a single definition for innovation, workshop participants generally used the term in a way that focused on the processes and mechanisms for producing commercial applications of new knowledge rather than on the products or outputs from these processes. The workshop discussions implied the following sort of working definition:

> Innovation is the transformation of knowledge into products, processes, systems, and services, with the key elements of underlying innovation being: (1) knowledge; (2) a skilled workforce; and (3) infrastructure.[3]

There was broad support in the workshop for the proposition that innovation drives manufacturing and other productivity growth, which in turn drives economic growth and national well-being. The PFI program seeks to connect, at the project and programmatic level, knowledge creation to innovation, and innovation to wealth, economic development, and, ultimately, national well-being.

---

[2]The viewpoints reported here were those expressed by workshop participants and do not necessarily reflect the positions of the National Science Foundation or RAND.

[3]Definition suggested by John Hurt, PFI program officer.

Regarding the process of transforming new knowledge into innovation, a common view was that although there were few proven formulas for innovation, work at the seams—i.e., work that cuts across traditional disciplinary lines and across university-industry lines—was where the unexpected could be expected to happen, with the result being a more effective innovation process.

Most of the workshop discussions focused on the steps involved in establishing partnerships that can bring an invention into the commercial world. The commercial link in many respects was viewed as the most critical link. Characteristics of commercially useful research were seen to include uniqueness and responsiveness to industry and market needs. Simply identifying potential strategic partners was seen as perhaps the main challenge, largely because of imperfections in information markets: Potential customers for inventions (industry) and potential suppliers of inventions (universities) frequently know very little about one another or where they might find common cause.

Another potential challenge was ensuring the requisite level of compatibility of objectives between university and industry and mutual understanding of (and respect for) differences in objectives. Differences in institutional cultures, time horizons, and confidentiality needs, and the potential for disagreements over royalty shares from intellectual property, were seen to be particularly problematic. Access to a host of other resources—money, personnel, and infrastructure—also were seen as potential challenges. Attendees offered a number of suggestions to overcome these challenges, most of which aimed to improve communications in some fashion or change university policies that hindered the university's ability to contribute to innovation.

The final link in the innovation chain—the spread of benefits beyond the partnership and its immediate customers to the broader local, state, regional, and national economy—received less attention. Nevertheless, workshop participants suggested that localities, regions, states, or nations ultimately compete with one another, particularly in creating new technology clusters that could lead to high-quality jobs and other types of economic development, and that competitive advantages were an important consideration at this level. Nevertheless, it can be exceedingly difficult to establish direct connections be-tween a specific innovation and larger economic or societal effects.

PARTNERSHIPS

More often than not, workshop participants described genuine part-nerships as dynamic and growing relationships based upon shared interests, trust, and an evolving technical relationship. Participants saw these relationships as necessarily multifaceted, including senior researchers, students, business people, and others who could find common ground and purpose. Some argued that such partnerships were inherently long-term in nature, but a vocal minority argued that innovative partnerships typically lasted only until the original pur-pose (commercializing the innovation) was achieved, at which time the most innovative partners would move on to the next challenge.

Catalyzing partnerships with these characteristics was seen to be very challenging. Partnerships required a vision and performance goals and benchmarks, passionate and visionary leaders, and part-ners who were bound by an essential interdependency and shared commitment. Moreover, to achieve success these partners needed to identify their competitive advantages (and disadvantages), resolve potential intellectual property (IP) disputes, and develop and execute strategic business plans. Continued communication and conflict resolution also were needed once the commercial phase was under way. In short, workshop participants warned that many centrifugal forces can pull partnerships apart and only one—the shared com-mitment and interdependency of the partners—can hold them to-gether.

The workshop also addressed the sorts of infrastructure that can sustain and nurture the spread of innovative activity over the long term. Workshop deliberations described infrastructure of three gen-eral kinds: for developing human capital, for developing networks, and for providing direct support for the innovation enterprise.

- To educate and train human capital for the research enterprise—and the entrepreneurial aspects of innovation—workshop partic-ipants saw the requirement for an innovative educational pro-cess whose most important goal was to serve the student, to provide hands-on education, and then to recruit and retain the best young scientists and engineers.

- The intellectual capital and know-how embodied in young scientists and engineers, honed through advanced education and training, is embedded in social networks characterized by shared commitment and trust. Such networks can be built through extended interactions and problem-solving, and represent a form of social capital that, in some workshop participants' minds, seemed to be the most important type of infrastructure of all.

- Finally, a base of operational support is essential, because sustainable partnerships cannot exist without such support. Ultimately, this was viewed both as a resource issue—a diversified base of private investment—and as a physical place that can provide a context for incubation; technical, management, and administrative support; laboratory and other capacity; communications services; and reliable sources of capital. The importance of support for federal innovation programs from at least one key constituency—the Congress—also was seen as critical.

A final aim of the PFI program is to broaden the participation of all institutions and people in the innovation enterprise, including underrepresented and underserved institutions and individuals. Workshop participants seemed to agree that this can successfully be accomplished through a solicitation and selection process that rewards quality; none argued that by including such institutions technical standards would necessarily suffer.

IMPLICATIONS FOR THE NSF

Two major points affecting both the PFI program and NSF came out of the workshop.

First, there was nearly unanimous support for a formal evaluation of the PFI program by an independent, paid evaluator. Such an effort was viewed as being consistent both with the NSF's general commitment to evaluation as an aid to outcome-based management and with its specific obligations under the Government Performance and Results Act of 1993 (GPRA). According to participants, such an evaluation should focus on the most critical questions related to innovation and the partnerships and should provide outcome and process measures for individual projects and the program as a whole.[4]

Second, the workshop endorsed both an expanded NSF role in promoting innovation and partnerships through the PFI program and continued efforts by the NSF to further diversify and better exploit synergisms in its support for innovation. The presentations and workshop discussions evidenced substantial enthusiasm for the PFI and other NSF programs that support innovation and university-industry collaborative efforts, without favoring any particular model (e.g., PFI) over any other (e.g., Industry/University Cooperative Research Centers, or I/UCRCs).

However, the workshop left unaddressed a number of critically important strategic-level questions that the NSF should consider in current and future planning: How can the NSF refine its understanding of the relative effectiveness of its innovation programs in promoting its objectives? Which of the available programs and models is the most appropriate tool for the NSF to use under which circumstances? In what ways can (or should) the NSF exploit synergies between programs (e.g., partnerships that are incubated in an engineering research center (ERC) or I/UCRC)? In what ways can (or should) this mosaic of programs be considered together as a larger whole to ensure that the NSF's enterprise-wide portfolio of innovation-catalyzing programs matches its strategic intent and its presumed desire to achieve an optimal program mix and level of diversification? What is the best balance or tradeoff among the various potentially conflicting imperatives (e.g., education and workforce development, academic research, innovation, and diversity)? What factors are associated with the success or failure of technology partnerships, networks, and clusters?

Insofar as these questions seems to be at the heart of the NSF's effort to build a new foundation for innovation in the new century while remaining true to its historical purpose, they are particularly deserving of further analysis, discussion, and debate.

---

[4]One reviewer of this report suggested that another way to categorize the metrics for evaluation would be in terms of input, output, outcome, and in-process metrics.

ACKNOWLEDGMENTS

We would like to thank Bruce Don, Michael Hynes, Athar Osama, Parry Norling, Steven Popper, and Caroline Wagner of RAND for their time and comments. We also would like to thank Terry West for developing a web-based survey form for collecting comments on the workshop, Phyllis Gilmore for developing web pages for the proceedings from the workshop, and Joe Hendrickson and Deborah Wesley for their assistance with data and analysis. We would like to thank John Hurt, Program Officer for the PFI program; members of the PFI Steering Committee; and the speakers, discussants, facilitators, resource people, rapporteurs, grantees and other attendees, and all of the others who made the workshop possible. We would also like to thank Kristin Leuschner and Patricia Bedrosian for their expert editorial assistance.

EHR	Education and Human Resources
EPSCoR	Experimental Program to Stimulate Competitive Research
ERC	Engineering Research Center
GOALI	Grant Opportunities for Academic Liaison with Industry program
GPRA	Government Performance and Results Act of 1993
H-1	Work visa
HP	Hewlett-Packard
IBM	International Business Machines
IP	Intellectual Property
I/UCRC	Industry/University Cooperative Research Centers
K–12	Kindergarten through 12th grade
NSF	National Science Foundation
PFI	Partnerships for Innovation
PI	Principal Investigator
R&D	Research and Development
REU	Research Experiences for Undergraduates

SBIR   Small Business Innovative Research program

S&T   Science and Technology

UCRC   University Cooperative Research Center

Chapter One

INTRODUCTION

The National Science Foundation (NSF) was created at the onset of the Cold War in 1950 "to promote the progress of science; to advance the national health, prosperity, and welfare; to secure the national defense; and for other purposes."[1] Consistent with this mission, the NSF is authorized by law to initiate and support both basic scientific research and applied research, programs to strengthen scientific and engineering research potential, science and engineering education programs at all levels, and an information base for science and engineering appropriate for development of national and international policy.[2]

Much has changed since the NSF's founding. There have been enormous changes in the international arena, as the imperative of military competition has largely been supplanted by that of economic competition. So too have changes occurred in the domestic arena, as a decade or more of "creative destruction" has transformed the U.S. manufacturing and service components of the economy.[3] And the challenges ahead—among them ensuring a workforce that is adequate in size, composition, and skills to support the level of economic growth and vitality that will be necessary as the ranks of retirees swell with the retirement of the baby boomers—are formidable ones. Last, the nature of the innovation enterprise also continues to

---

[1]The NSF's continuing mission is set out in the preamble to the National Science Foundation Act of 1950 (Public Law 810507).

[2]National Science Foundation (2001), p. 1.

[3]The phrase "creative destruction" is credited to the economist Joseph A. Schumpeter. For an example of the use of the concept in the area of innovation, see Stein (1997).

change, with the result that industry shoulders an increasingly large share of the burden for research and development (R&D), and the federal government's share has shrunk.[4]

For the NSF, these changes have motivated an increased focus on ideas, innovation, and managing knowledge as a critical resource—the drivers of productivity and economic growth.[5] Moreover, changes in the innovation process itself call for a different set of tools and institutional arrangements to be effective.

In recognition of these changes, the NSF recently developed a vision—"enabling the nation's future through discovery, learning, and innovation"— to supplement its longstanding statutory mission and to highlight the centrality of innovation in that mission.[6]

NSF support for innovation is not new: Traditionally, the NSF's role in the national innovation system has been to provide funding for basic research to gain new knowledge, education, and training for the current and future workforce, and infrastructure that serves as the foundation for research. The NSF likes to say that it supports people (education and workforce development), ideas (gaining knowledge that can lead to innovations), and tools (infrastructure).[7] It does so by supporting the development of intellectual capital, integrating research and education, and promoting partnerships.

Of the three main types of research and development collaboration—industry-led consortia, collaborations between universities and industry, and collaborations between industry and federal laboratories—the NSF's mission statement dictates a focus on universities by virtue of their role as centers of research, development, and training. The NSF always has had a close association with universities and has traditionally been able to achieve many of its goals through these institutions. As the NSF's goals have evolved to meet the nation's changing needs—including those of the national inno-

---

[4]See for example, Hicks et al. (2001).

[5]Stein (1997).

[6]The importance of basic research on a use-inspired basis and the view that the linear R&D model is no longer valid are discussed in Stokes (1997).

[7]From Bordogna (2000).

vation system and broader economy—NSF has sought to develoμ new ways to achieve its goals through universities.[8]

Although the NSF historically has supported collaborative researcl programs that linked universities, industry, and governments, thes‹ efforts were greatly expanded beginning with the university-industr₁ Cooperative Research program in the 1970s, during the 1980s witʰ the creation of Engineering Research Centers (ERCs), and in th‹ 1990s with the Grant Opportunities for Academic Liaison witʰ Industry (GOALI) program. The NSF's model of university-industr₁ partnerships has been widely emulated by other federal agencies.[9]

The NSF today supports more than 100 university centers, including Industry/University Cooperative Research Centers (I/UCRCs), State-I/UCRCs, Engineering Research Centers, Materials Research Science and Engineering Centers, Science and Technology Centers, and Minority Research Centers of Excellence, as well as GOALI, supporting links between university students and their counterparts in industry, and Experimental Program to Stimulate Competitive Research (EPSCoR). Total NSF activity involving industry was estimated in 1999 to be about $1 billion, nearly a quarter of the NSF's overall budget.[10]

Smaller firms and institutions have become increasingly important to the national innovation system over the last decade,[11] necessitating a greater focus on innovation at the micro-level. Meanwhile, adverse demographic trends that may result in a smaller future workforce and a larger population of pensioners demands investments that can continue to yield productivity increases and economic

---

[8]This discussion focuses on NSF's role in innovation and partnerships, but a broad literature exists on these topics. For additional reading, see American Council on Education (2001) and Government-University-Industry Research Roundtable (1999).

[9]Mowery (1998).

[10]De Graaf (1999). There are currently 25 NSF Science and Technology Centers.

[11]For example, between 1989 and 1997, the percentage of industrial research and development performed by firms with fewer than 500 employees increased from 7.7 to 15.5 percent, while the percentage performed by firms of 25,000 or more employees fell from 76 to 66 percent. See National Science Board (2000), Vol. 2, Table 2-53, p. A-95. Between 1992 and 1999, the percentage of academic research and development performed by the top 10 institutions fell from 19.3 to 18.1 percent of all academic R&D. National Science Foundation (1999).

opportunities the NSF should consider in promoting university-industry and other partnerships in programs such as the PFI.

To paraphrase one breakout session: "We need to measure innovation, and partnerships." Accordingly, following Chapter Two, which provides an overview of the PFI program and the June 2001 workshop, Chapters Three and Four report workshop discussions related to these two topics and their measurement, and most of Chapter Five summarizes workshop recommendations regarding an evaluation of the PFI program and the NSF's role in supporting innovation. A number of appendixes also are provided containing relevant background information on the workshop and the partnerships.

Throughout most of this material—Chapter Two through most of Chapter Five—our aim has been to faithfully report, summarize, and synthesize, without critiquing or implying endorsement by RAND or the National Science Foundation, the viewpoints expressed by workshop participants. We relied on the notes of rapporteurs in each breakout session, plenary presentations by breakout session chairs, and a transcript of the plenary sessions as our main source material. We restructured this material thematically and provided connecting threads—or occasional references to other material—to improve context or flow, or where it otherwise seemed warranted. At the end of Chapter Five we share our own views but only in the limited context of identifying what we feel to be the main questions that the NSF will need to address as it considers its future role in catalyzing innovation.

Chapter Two

OVERVIEW OF THE PFI PROGRAM AND THE WORKSHOP

The Partnerships for Innovation program was created in FY 2000 as a result of a Congressional appropriation of $8.5 million to initiate a new innovation partnership effort.[1] On March 10, 2000, a PFI planning workshop was held to develop a shared understanding of the concepts of "innovation" and "partnerships for innovation" including specific examples; to provide guidance for the PFI solicitation; and to identify future actions, such as the workshop held in June 2001, to advance the PFI initiative.[2] The findings from the planning workshop, in addition to input from NSF staff, led to the creation of the PFI program solicitation shortly thereafter.

THE PROGRAM SOLICITATION

The program solicitation called for proposals for partnerships among universities, government, and the private sector that would explore new approaches to support and sustain innovation in the long term. Degree-granting academic institutions of higher learning were to serve as lead institutions or partners, in that they were responsible for the overall management of the proposed partnership. At a minimum, the partnership was to include an academic institution and a private sector organization. In addition, other academic institutions, private sector firms (including entrepreneurs and venture capital-

---

[1] See NSF Section of Public Law 106-74, VA/HUD and Other Independent Agencies Act for FY 2000 at http://www.nsf.gov/od/lpa/congress/106/106majorleg.htm.

[2] From Bordogna (2000).

ists), state/local government entities, and nonprofit/trade/profes-
sional associations could be involved.

Eligibility limitations were such that degree-granting academic institutions of higher learning could participate in no more than two
partnership proposals and could serve as the lead for only one. A
senior institutional administrator (dean or higher) in the lead institution was to serve as the co- or principal investigator of the proposal.
The proposed partnerships were to request total budgets ranging
from $300,000 to $600,000 for the award's duration of two to three
years.

THE REVIEW PROCESS

A total of 130 proposals were submitted for consideration in the first
year (2000). The NSF solicited reviews of these proposals from peers
with expertise in the substantive area of the proposed project, with
the reviewers selected by program officers charged with the oversight
of the review process. The NSF invited each applicant to suggest, at
the time of submission, the names of appropriate or inappropriate
reviewers. Care was taken to ensure that reviewers had no conflicts
with the proposer. Special efforts were made to recruit reviewers
from nonacademic institutions, minority-serving institutions, or ad-
jacent disciplines to that principally addressed in the proposal.

Proposals were reviewed against the following general review criteria
established by the National Science Board:

- What is the intellectual merit of the proposed activity? How important is the proposed activity to advancing knowledge and understanding within its own field or across different fields? How
  well qualified is the proposer (individual or team) to conduct the
  project? To what extent does the proposed activity suggest and
  explore creative and original concepts? How well conceived and
  organized is the proposed activity? Is there sufficient access to
  resources?

- What are the broader effects of the proposed activity? How well
  does the activity advance discovery and understanding while
  promoting teaching, training, and learning? How well does the
  proposed activity broaden the participation of underrepresented

groups (e.g., women, minorities, the disabled, or those in particular geographic areas)? To what extent will it enhance the infrastructure for research and education, such as facilities, instrumentation, networks, and partnerships? Will the results be disseminated broadly to enhance scientific and technological understanding? What will the benefits of the proposed activity to society be?

Principal investigators also were asked to address the following elements in their proposal to provide reviewers with the information necessary to respond fully to both of the above-described NSF merit review criteria:

- *Integration of Research and Education.* One principal strategy in support of the NSF's goals is to foster integration of research and education through the programs, projects, and activities it supports at academic and research institutions. These institutions provide abundant opportunities where individuals may concurrently assume responsibilities as researchers, educators, and students and where all can engage in joint efforts that infuse education with the excitement of discovery and enrich research through the diversity of learning perspectives.

- *Integrating Diversity into NSF Programs, Projects, and Activities.* Broadening opportunities and enabling the participation of all citizens—including women, underrepresented minorities, and persons with disabilities—are essential to the health and vitality of science and engineering. The NSF is committed to this principle of diversity and deems it central to the programs, projects, and activities it considers and supports.

The following additional PFI-specific review criteria also were used:

- Responsiveness of the proposal to the goals of the PFI program;

- The degree to which the proposed activity will stimulate new innovation opportunities for the partner organizations;

- The potential effect of the proposed innovation activities on the economic or societal well-being of the region,

- Potential of the proposed partnership to foster and sustain innovation in the long term;

- The degree to which institutions that serve groups currently underrepresented in the science, engineering, and technological workforce participate in the proposed innovation activity; and

- The degree to which institutions that serve regions or sectors not yet fully participating in the innovation enterprise contribute to the proposed activities.

In addition to these criteria, in making the final award decisions the NSF also considered geographic distribution and diversity of lead institutions, the likely distribution of societal effects, and the distribution of technology or industry sectors served.

All proposals were reviewed by at least three reviewers outside the NSF who were experts in the particular field represented by the proposal. Reviewers were asked to formulate a recommendation to either support or decline each proposal. The program officer assigned to manage the proposal's review considered the advice of reviewers and formulated a recommendation.

THE PARTNERSHIPS

Of the 130 proposals submitted in the first year, the PFI program awarded grants to 24 promising partnerships that aimed to translate knowledge gained from basic research into new products, businesses, and services; to provide workforce education and training opportunities focused on innovation; and to develop infrastructure that would support future innovation.[3]

To provide a better sense of the composition of these partnerships, Table 2.1 shows that all 24 university awardees partnered with industry, although some also partnered with others from universities, or from government, from the venture capital community, or from incubators. And Table 2.2 reports that with 20 partnerships citing it as a major goal, technology transfer was by far the most frequently identified major goal in these partnerships, followed by education

---

[3]National Science Foundation (2000). Descriptions of these partnerships can be found in Appendix B. In its second year (2001), 109 proposals were submitted; the NSF recommended funding for 12 partnerships.

useful research, the principal challenges and barriers to commercial-ization, and the means for eliminating these barriers, discussed next.

Characteristics of Commercially Useful Research

There was general agreement on a number of key points regarding the characteristics of commercially useful research:[10]

- *Uniqueness.* Rather than thinking in terms of "research" or "development,"[11] commercially useful research was envisaged in terms of creative ideas that could lead to a new product or process, increased performance or cost-effectiveness for an existing one, or some other improvement. Key characteristics of innovative research included unique features or a proprietary advantage over the present state of the art.

- *Industry-Driven.* Participants saw commercially useful research as being industry-driven in the sense of meeting the needs of companies working on a specific area of technology application by providing research that can improve a product or process.

- *Market-Driven.* There was general agreement that a key charac-teristic of commercially useful research was that it needed to meet a real need and offer a sufficiently high payoff or return on investment in terms of commercial benefit to justify the potentially high risk. Whether the research yielded incremental or discontinuous change or was directed at a narrow or niche market or a broad industry or regional market, it required an identified end user and customer and market receptivity. This in turn necessitated both a tangible benefit (e.g., a new capability, increased performance, cost reduction) and a capacity to capture the payoff rapidly enough to meet company or industry time frames. Participants argued that if a commercial entity was willing to provide resources, the research was by definition

---

[10]For additional reading on when partnerships can be valuable, see Roberts and Berry (1985). For additional reading on criteria for building a successful business, see O'Brien and Fadem (1999).

[11]This was captured in a question asked by one of the breakout sessions: "Is it 'Research,' 'Development,' or 'Innovation'?"

commercially viable but, over the long term, a market was needed to support the research.[12]

Principal Challenges or Barriers to Commercialization

A number of challenges or barriers were identified throughout the commercialization process.[13]

First, simply identifying strategic partners represented a potential challenge for both university and industry actors. This seemed to be tied to the belief that university researchers frequently did not know which firms might benefit most from application of their research. On the industry side, many firms did not fully understand the worth of research, how to integrate it into company operations, or—particularly in the case of smaller firms—which researchers were working in relevant technology areas.[14]

Another potential challenge was ensuring the requisite level of compatibility of objectives, and mutual understanding of (and respect for) differences in the objectives of different partners:

- On the one hand, universities and industry were seen to have very different institutional cultures and motivations that could, without adequate recognition and attention, disrupt an otherwise productive partnership. For example, because the planning horizons for companies are typically shorter than those for university researchers, time-to-market often can be a problem: It can be difficult to get work done for a company quickly in an academic environment, since academic research by definition

---

[12]There also were two "minority opinions" on this subject. First, some held that university researchers should identify problems and solutions rather than seeking to find technology that was commercially viable; in this view, commercialization simply was not the business of universities. In a similar vein, some felt that commercially successful applications had little educational value for students. Still another view was that university researchers would be placed in an undesirable (subordinate) role by being too closely tied to commercialization. See Ember (2000) and Wasserman (2000).

[13]The innovation process is filled with risks: Studies have shown that it takes 3,000 raw ideas, out of which over 300 novel ideas are identified, to produce one significant commercial success. See Stevens and Burley (1997).

[14]This recognition occasioned a number of ideas about how best to perform the necessary "matchmaking," discussed below.

takes longer. At the same time, the university has a longer-term focus with respect to both research and education. Although participants felt that the business community as a whole understands today better than ever that training the workforce is important and that good technological skills are needed, this appreciation may not find expression in all firm partnerships with universities.

- On the other hand, potential friction was seen to arise because universities and industry often were seen to be after precisely the same thing—e.g., financial returns from the exploitation of intellectual property (IP) rights. Universities increasingly have been seeking to capture financial rewards from their IP, to the point where the issue has become a source of friction in industry-university relationships. Two recurring topics in the workshop were the need to clarify intellectual property issues to reduce these sources of potential friction and the need for universities to look beyond financial returns on their IP that could yield important benefits (e.g., entrepreneurial experience, training and workforce development, or new lab equipment) by crafting creative win-win arrangements, rather than inciting disagreements over how to fairly divide royalties.

- In a similar vein, industry partners frequently want to keep projects confidential as long as possible, whereas university partners want to publish results as quickly and widely as possible.[15]

Access to various types of resources also was seen as a potential barrier:

- *Money.* The availability of capital was seen as an important potential barrier to commercialization, although it also was seen as a potential area of company advantage, since companies typically had at least some money that they could use to locate or seed academic partners.

- *Personnel.* Participants recognized the challenge of developing or attracting experienced and skilled personnel in all roles and at all levels of the innovation enterprise. These included accom-

---

[15]See Behrens and Gray (2001).

plished leaders who could construct, articulate, promote, and coordinate execution of a coherent vision and carry it through the commercialization process; managers who had the necessary business acumen and experience in integrating R&D and business, and bringing technologies to market; and the right number and mix of people in the right location to ensure successful product or process development.

- *Infrastructure.* In a similar vein, the lack of infrastructure, including administration and management support, was seen as a potential barrier to successful commercialization of research.

Means for Eliminating Barriers

Of the various challenges to commercialization that workshop attendees identified, perhaps the greatest amount of attention was devoted to improving the chances that prospective university and industry partners would be able to find one another.

There appeared to be numerous opportunities to improve communications between potential academic and industry partners that could facilitate the identification of potential matches and create new opportunities for partnerships. Among the means that were discussed were encouraging a variety of outreach activities that would bring together the academic and business communities, public reporting of research activities to improve industry awareness of potentially useful research, and the development by universities of marketing or sales strategies that target industries with information about researchers performing potentially useful research.

Also viewed as important were changes to university and industry reward systems and incentives; without the proper incentives, some argued, efforts to bridge the university-industry gap could be expected to remain smaller than desired. Among the changes that were suggested were revised university policies on promotion decisions that would give greater weight to patenting and other innovative activity and tax credits for industry partners that could promote greater efforts by industry to find university partners. Efforts to speed up the patent cycle and time-to-market and those aimed at improving knowledge management practices to facilitate the diffusion of practical knowledge also were seen as important means of eliminating existing barriers to commercialization.

Measurement Issues

Outcome Measures. The project-level outcome measures that related to the successful commercialization of an innovative application focused predominantly on indicators that an innovative application was being used and yielding commercial rewards. These included the number of licenses/licensees, revenue from licenses and royalties, equity positions, initial public offerings, buyouts, sales, and jobs created.

At the program level, a number of suggested outcome measures addressed the broader question, "Has the overall PFI contributed to innovation?" Most of these were viewed simply as summations of the project-level outcome measures related to innovation that were identified earlier, such as the total number of patents for all projects supported by the PFI program over some period of time.

Signposts. Signposts for this step included meetings between researchers and industry partners, meetings between partners and potential customers, other expressions of commercial interest in the innovation, as well as the actual provision of startup funding or other commitments by industry partners or customers.

FROM WEALTH TO NATIONAL WELL-BEING

The final link in the commercial innovation chain involves the spread of benefits beyond the partnership and its immediate customers to the broader local, state, regional, and national economies. This was viewed as taking place as a result of expansion of the innovative enterprise that is the focus of the partnership and the expansion of firms or industries that may benefit from the innovation. It also could happen by virtue of productivity improvements that result from the innovation.

Considering Comparative (and Competitive) Advantages

Workshop participants suggested the potential for localities, regions, states, or nations to compete with one another, particularly in creating new technology clusters that could lead to high-quality jobs and other types of economic development in the same way that comparative and competitive advantage play in commercial markets.[16]

- At the regional level, it was seen as important to mobilize the intellectual and economic resources resident in the region to realize the opportunity in key emerging technology sectors to build a sustainable regional economy and to compete with other regional clusters.[17]

- At the state level, it was noted that many states have the same sorts of objectives in fostering regional development based upon private sector investment in technology industries. These states essentially compete with one another for private and other investment. This sort of competition requires that a partnership consider broader economic development strategies that include private sector entrepreneurs to establish the comparative advantages of one state over another. This issue also raised important questions about the roles of the private and public sector, how universities educate and train the workforce, and how the state can provide some of the infrastructure that can confer competitive advantage.[18]

- More broadly still, some argued that it was important to integrate across regions and not to rely solely on educational institutions within a specific area or state; developing partnerships from

---

[16]On technology clusters, see Swann, Prevezer, and Stout (1998) and Saxenian (1996). A reason for clustering is offered by Wolfgang Keller: Technology diffusion is severely limited by distance. See Keller (2001).

[17]For example, one partnership saw Research Triangle Park and the Richmond and Northern Virginia areas as potential regional competitors.

[18]Analyses of state-based science and technology parks suggest that this might not always be the case. An analysis of Research Triangle Park and University of Utah Research Park showed that the former aimed to attract talent and investment mainly from out of state and the latter focused on providing incentives to faculty, students, and state residents to develop high-technology businesses in the state, with both finding success. See Luger and Goldstein (1991).

within the network of former students and a broader network abroad was suggested as one way of doing this. Some even argued that networking enabled competitors to become collaborators, in which case geography would not matter as much.

Measurement Issues

Outcome Measures. Some attendees argued that project-level outcome measures should include micro-level economic outcomes such as partnership-related jobs created, although again the distinction between the micro- and macro-levels was not always clear, and participants recognized that there are inherent difficulties in their estimation.

Whether the level of analysis is an individual partnership, a network, a locality, a state, or a region, measuring economic effects relies on analyses that compare observed outcomes (e.g., jobs created) with some estimate of the baseline level of economic performance that would have obtained in a counterfactual world where the PFI project did not exist. In this world, the partners might (or might not) still have met with some level of commercial success, with some level of broader economic benefit resulting. Ascertaining the "value added" from a project is therefore quite difficult, since success is a nonnormal random variable and because of the complexity and looming uncertainties in counterfactual analyses.[19]

Thus, if the assessment of micro-level economic effects was viewed as a difficult proposition, participants viewed as tough to impossible the task of reliably assessing macro-level economic effects. For the most part, this was because of the same sorts of problems that plagued the micro-level analyses of economic effect: understanding outcomes that derived from complex economic processes both in the observed world and in a counterfactual one. In a broader (state or regional) setting, the number of potential confounding factors—and the uncertainties—grew. Of course, to the extent that the range of effects could be bounded, they could be treated as summative and

---

[19]For example, see BankBoston's effort to relate "MIT-related" companies to jobs and sales. BankBoston Economics Department (1997).

aggregated to estimate the range of potential economic effects for the PFI program as a whole.[20]

Signposts. No distinctions were made between the outcome measures and the principal signposts for gauging broader economic effects.

CONCLUSIONS

This chapter has provided a synthesis of workshop discussions regarding the various phases of innovation. It suggested, first, that innovation appeared to be most likely at the seams between disciplines, technologies, and institutions, with strong implications for the characteristics of the sorts of partnerships that should be nurtured, a subject that is taken up in greater detail in the next chapter. It also suggested that commercialization was the essential process by which innovations can lead to wealth and that the commercial considerations are the preeminent ones determining the stream of benefits that may flow from an innovation. It also suggested the process by which commercial innovations can have broader economic effects, on productivity, for example, or job growth, although the direct connections can be exceedingly difficult to establish. The next chapter shifts the focus to workshop discussions regarding partnerships.

---

[20]See, for example, Salter and Martin (2001), which concludes that no simple model of the economic benefits from basic research is possible. For additional reading, see Griliches (1991, 1995) and Mansfield (1991a, 1991b). Both have attempted to develop estimates of return from basic research to society.

Chapter Four

CATALYZING PARTNERSHIPS TO ENABLE INFRASTRUCTURE AND BROADEN PARTICIPATION

When we first set about designing the PFI program, we had many hours of lively debate about how it should be structured. What guidelines should we develop for prospective grantees? What parameters should we require of the partnerships? We all knew that PFI would best serve its purpose if it attracted a wide variety of institutions, partnerships, and proposed experiments and innovation.

In the end, we decided to place very few restrictions in the proposal description. We wanted to provide the maximum freedom possible for grantees to be innovative about innovation. . . . We've reached out to find the capable people with the best ideas to begin the extraordinary process of transforming our innovation system to meet the needs of the 21st Century.

Joseph Bordogna, Deputy Director, National Science Foundation

To paraphrase one breakout session's plenary report: "The PFI aims to catalyze innovation, and partnerships are how we go about doing that." This chapter accordingly describes workshop discussions regarding three further aims of the PFI program that are related to partnerships and their growth: catalyzing partnerships, catalyzing enabling infrastructure, and broadening participation in the national innovation enterprise.

CATALYZING PARTNERSHIPS FOR INNOVATION

More often than not, workshop participants described genuine partnerships as dynamic and growing relationships based upon shared interests, trust, and an evolving technical relationship.[1] Participants described these relationships as necessarily multifaceted, including senior researchers, students, business people, and others who could find common ground and purpose, and as long term in nature.

Attendees identified a number of characteristics that were associated with successful partnerships that can be thought of in terms of discrete steps. These steps incorporate both broad issues of the partnership's ends and narrower ones of means, ultimately leading to a fuller understanding of the essential interdependency of all partners.[2] Although the following discussion suggests a top-down—and sequential—process, there is obvious concurrency and interdependency among the steps.

Establishing a Vision

First, successful partnerships have a vision that provides an image of what constitutes success in fairly concrete terms (e.g., an incremental innovation that can improve a product or process or a radical innovation that can enable a new one).[3] This can provide a basis for further specifying goals and objectives, for establishing a roadmap for realizing the vision, and for providing incentives to agents of change.

Workshop attendees placed a great deal of emphasis on the development of a vision for each partnership, one that in many cases would be the work of a single champion who could provide the lead-

---

[1]Participants in one breakout session contrasted a partnership in which the parties want the partnership to grow and sustain itself with a "marriage of convenience" in which one party just wants something (e.g., money). Mowery (1998) describes key elements of collaborations and proposes features that are associated with better performance.

[2]Some participants even believed that there was a cyclical component in the partnership process: As initial goals were achieved, members of the partnership would establish new ones.

[3]As E. Roger Novak of Venture Capital for Partnerships put it in his talk: "Ideas are plentiful, visions are powerful."

ership and overall coordination necessary to ensure that the partnership was a success. This vision would need to set a tone that embraced the most important aspirations of all of the partners, while providing a coherent statement of the overall end state to which the partnership itself aspired.

Establishing Performance Goals and Benchmarks

There was broad agreement that the partnership's vision needed to be supplemented by a definition of measurable outcomes and benefits of the partnership that could be used to establish benchmarks and to measure progress.[4]

Clear, achievable measures are needed to assess goal performance (e.g., results and return on investment) and these should include measures that speak to the quality of relationships in the partnership. The metrics should point to the desired end-state for the partnership, which some argued should provide the basis for an "exit strategy" that plans for the obsolescence of the current project and a path to the next one.[5]

Identifying Leaders

To realize the partnership's vision and to make it operational, a visionary and passionate leader is needed. This leader must either be brought in or cultivated from within the partnership.[6] In either case, because passionate leaders are rare, expensive, and in high demand, money must be available to pay whatever the market will bear for their services.[7] The frequency with which the topic of leadership arose suggested that many participants doubted whether a partner-

---

[4]We will return to the question of performance measures in the next chapter.

[5]This could involve either a focus on a new area or incremental improvements (line extensions) to an existing line.

[6]According to some, the self-interest of all parties was important in both the short and long term, whereas champions (organizations and people) were needed for the long term.

[7]Many seemed to argue that the leader generally would precede and lead the development of a partnership, but the possibility of a leader emerging from within the partnership also was recognized.

ship could even survive without one or more vibrant leaders who could champion the partnership's cause.

A recurring theme in the discussions related to the broadening of discrete partnerships to larger networks and clusters was the need for strong local leaders from relevant professional communities (e.g., university, industry, venture capital, the law). These leaders had to be both influential and powerfully committed to the region, capable of knitting together all of the elements that were necessary to ensure a high probability of success: strategic and business plans, private capital, broader institutional and community support, and other elements. They also needed to be capable of building and managing the partnership and selling the partnership to the outside world (e.g., potential investors, the community, the state).

Recruiting Committed Partners

As suggested above, the core of a successful partnership was conceived of as comprising the minimal set of partners needed to provide all of the competencies and resources—an innovative idea, leadership, one or more technological approaches to its realization, entrepreneurial and marketing skills, administrative and financial support, and so on—to bring an innovation to market.

The overarching aim in finding partners was to identify other parties with common strategic interests and complementary strengths and weaknesses:

- For universities, this often meant looking for industry partners with equipment, infrastructure, or other needed resources—not necessarily financial ones[8]—who might be able to implement research.

- For industry, the aim was finding academic partners who had relevant know-how that could make a contribution to a joint venture.

---

[8]Indeed, some participants felt that academics who were going after money were going down the wrong path.

For purposes of building the partnership, this necessitates a three-step process for building shared commitment based upon mutual understanding and appreciation:

- *Mutual Understanding.* Successful partnerships were characterized by candor and mutual understanding of individual partners' principal reasons for involvement in the partnership, including their motives, goals, and needs; the compatibility (or potential incompatibility) of partners' interests; comparative strengths and weaknesses, resources, and constraints; and roles and responsibilities of each member of the partnership.[9]

- *Mutual Appreciation Based on Interdependency.* The mutual understanding found in genuine partnerships and the alignment of roles and responsibilities based upon an understanding of comparative strengths and weaknesses of the partners led to an interdependency that was viewed as healthy and essential for the partnership.   If partners did not really need one another to accomplish the partnership's goals, some averred, then they should go elsewhere. A partnership meant that a partner really could not go anywhere else to accomplish his goals.

- *Shared Commitment.* In successful partnerships, it was critical that the interdependency and essential need for the capabilities of other partners just described be accompanied by shared commitment—all partners need to be highly motivated and deeply involved in the partnership.[10]

A network of committed customers and other stakeholders and supporters also must be developed, providing positive feedback and support for joint ventures. Customers and other stakeholders and supporters at all levels must be continually engaged and apprised of the status of progress.

University Strategies for Finding Partners. A number of elements of potential university strategies for finding partners were identified:

---

[9]A prominent subject was ensuring a level of candor among partners to reveal their true motives rather than claiming purely altruistic ones.

[10]Words such as "driven" were used to describe the nature of the partners' commitment, and partnerships were said to require "a sense of urgency in the strategic sense—something needs to happen."

- "Partnership friendly" university policies were seen to make a big difference in attracting industry partners, with universities having such policies able to advertise these policies to attract industry partners;

- Multidisciplinary science, technology, and business centers and university-industry institutes were seen as excellent indicators of a "partnership friendly" environment that could provide a potentially effective and efficient liaison between the university and potential industry partners;[11]

- Technology transfer offices can evangelize the university's endowments in science and technology, including its skilled science and engineering workforce, and both senior researchers and graduate students;

- In light of the belief that universities need to understand an industry to target it, universities can conduct industry needs assessments and capacity assessments to ascertain what type of technologies are needed and commercially viable and where university researchers can add the most value;

- In relatively mature areas of technology, university researchers can identify firms with the most patents in an area;[12]

- Networks (such as alumni networks) were seen as a source of potential industry partners who would be sympathetic to joint ventures with university researchers; such networks should be encouraged and used by universities;

- Showcases and industrial research fairs were viewed as potentially powerful ways of drawing companies to university events and presenting opportunities for researchers to interact with firm representatives; such showcases could be coupled with projects that yielded models or pilot demonstrations that had potential for industry application.

---

[11]On industry-university collaborations, see Industrial Research Institute (1996).

[12]This approach was believed unlikely to work as well in emerging technology areas and markets.

Industry Strategies for Finding Partners. Also described were a number of potential industry strategies for finding academic partners:

- Industry searches can focus on universities with technology transfer offices, multidisciplinary industry-oriented "centers of excellence," universities with "partnership friendly" policies, or those that have many patents or citations in an area of interest;

- Concentrating on identifying multidisciplinary centers of excellence or university-industry research centers that focus on the science, engineering, and technologies underlying a specific industry appeared to be a more profitable approach than focusing at the university level; similarly, focusing on schools with department-level reputation and expertise and those that educated particularly valuable employees were seen as potentially useful strategies;

- Individual professors doing work in relevant areas can be identified by reputation or by their publishing record; these academic researchers could be engaged on specific technological problems or challenges and invited to submit informal proposals;

- Industrial fairs were seen as a way of getting academics out of their departments and providing a basis for evaluating their performance and the prospects that they might contribute materially to solving an industry challenge;

- Some firms simply show up at a research institution and see what research has been done and what can be used;

- Firms can use a consultant to find the best universities for work in a specific area;

- Firms can use employees who are former graduate students as an interface between the business and universities;

- Representatives of firms can attend meetings of professional and technical societies;

- Finally, the internet can be used to conduct searches of universities and their expertise.[13]

Identifying Comparative and Competitive Advantages

Although there seemed to be agreement that the broader market environment narrows viable areas of research, participants felt that the partnerships should aim to shape that environment. To accomplish this, partnerships need to be guided by a systematic appraisal of their own strengths and weaknesses relative to other commercial efforts that goes well beyond the stock-taking of individual partners' strengths and weaknesses. The partnership needs to identify its comparative and competitive advantages over other technology development and industry efforts, whether in the larger context of an existing market, product, or process, or an entirely new one.

According to workshop participants, this appraisal should include a sort of market analysis that identifies customers, competitors, products, processes, and underlying technologies in the area in which the partnership hopes to compete and identifies the unique characteristics of the partnership's efforts that will make it competitive. A clear view of the market and potential competitors in that market also was seen as a characteristic of successful partnerships. If a partnership had some things that were unique and different from its competitors, then it could successfully compete and take advantage of individual partners' expertise.[14] The partnership also should identify any remaining elements (e.g., public relations, marketing) that will be needed to bring the innovation to market, particularly if it is an area outside the experience and expertise of existing partners.

---

[13]For examples, see Yet2.com, which acts as a broker of technologies, and www. ninesigma.com, which has developed a way to find out who is doing research in what areas and can lead those interested in getting research done for them to proper scientists.

[14]Workshop participants appear to have taken a broad view of the market: A market could be a particular locality or industry niche, an entire industry, or a regional economy that was competing with other regional economies.

Resolving Intellectual Property Issues[15]

IP is the mechanism by which the benefits of an innovation are appropriated (owned) by one or more parties; in general, because industry is driven by the profit motive, historically it has sought to exploit intellectual property to a greater extent than have universities (see the box, below).

The disposition of intellectual property—for purposes of workshop participants, primarily patented inventions[16]—generally revolved around three key questions: Who owns and is the assignee on the IP? Who controls and has the right to commercialize, sell, or otherwise use the IP? Who benefits through a share in the profits made from the use of the IP? In short, it is the property rights associated with the intellectual property, and not the question of who invented it, that is crucial. In a standard university-industry collaboration, three other questions also typically arise: When can the academic partner publish? What level of confidentiality must be maintained in the academic environment? And what is the overhead rate?

There was broad agreement among workshop participants that the benefits to researchers of intellectual property were not exclusively—nor even necessarily primarily—in terms of financial sponsorship, opportunities for consulting, or the revenues that might result from licensing and patents. Indeed, a wide range of potential nonfinancial benefits of IP were cited, including internships for students and early recruitment of graduate students into industry, laboratory equipment and other "in-kind" benefits, and the potential treatment of patents as "publications" in performance reviews, promotion, and tenure decisions.[17]

---

[15]One breakout session focused on the issue of intellectual property, and a number of others touched upon the subject in their discussions.

[16]Intellectual property also includes copyrights and trademarks, but these were seen as less important for purposes of the workshop.

[17]Many of these benefits occur from partnerships in general. However, participants discussed at length the benefits that were observed when IP was also involved.

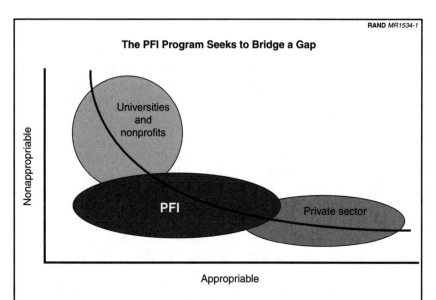

SOURCE: Hurt (2001). Figure created by Jere Denton and used with permission.

NOTES: The academic and nonprofit sectors engage in activities the fruits of which generally are not appropriated back to them. They produce knowledge as a public good in the form of students, publications, and other outputs that can contribute to societal well-being, but they do not generally seek—and often are not able—to appropriate benefits from these activities for themselves. By contrast, the private sector engages in commercial activities, where the benefits from intellectual property (know-how, revenues, profits, etc.) generally are appropriable. PFI aims to fill a gap between university and industry that can arise as a result of the university's need for new funding sources and industry's need for innovative new ideas and willingness to pay for them. It provides an opportunity for academic, nonprofit, and private sector actors to appropriate enough of the benefits to make the effort worthwhile and sustainable. For the university, those benefits may be in the form of consulting, internships and on-the-job training, funding, or lab equipment and other infrastructure. For the private sector, new sources of knowledge can be harnessed, and skilled scientists, engineers, and other workers can be put to work laying the foundations for emerging commercial opportunities and challenges.

Although the numerous benefits seemed clear to participants, also clear were the numerous issues that needed to be resolved by each member of the partnership to ensure that IP did not become a source of friction. Participants noted that there often were a host of unstated expectations in IP agreements (e.g., regarding the ownership, control, and benefits from IP) that equally often went unmet and became a source of friction between partners. The importance of symmetry in the benefits also was mentioned as a critical issue, since all parties needed to have a sufficiently substantial stake in the outcome to devote effort to achieving success. A lack of awareness regarding what IP issues needed to be worked out also was deemed to be an important source of problems.

Some argued that the main challenge to resolving IP issues was related to the communication necessary to bridge gaps between partners. For example, cultural differences that arise from different (e.g., academic, industrial, legal) backgrounds and perspectives were seen as important; universities need to see themselves as partners rather than owners of IP.[18] There also is a lack of awareness of the very different capabilities and needs of small and large businesses; small businesses were seen as needing to own IP to be attractive to others, for their own strategic planning purposes, and to avoid licensing and other costs, whereas large firms typically have law departments that established IP guidelines and have established ways of doing business with universities. The best means for resolving disagreements was, not surprisingly, fostering communication and mutual understanding among all involved organizations and parties. Placing time limits on the ownership of the IP also was seen as a means for reducing long-term risks among the agreeing parties. By limiting the ownership, partners would have the ability to renegotiate, at a fixed point, the various equities for that IP (partners would not be forever signing away their rights).

Further, there frequently were tensions between the ownership of the IP and the benefits derived from the IP; IP generated at academic institutions typically remains the property of the institution, but the

---

[18]For example, proprietary information, confidentiality requirements, and reliability and validity of data can mean different things to different people.

tax code limits the ability of nonprofit institutions funded with tax-exempt bonds to share in the financial profits of IP.[19] Of course, such restrictions generally do not apply to industry, but the result is nevertheless that most IP is either not commercialized at all or is underutilized, with no one gaining benefits from it.[20]

The institutional, cultural, and legal roots of these differences suggested that changes might be needed. There was recognition, for example, that in many universities a cultural change would be required to change the reward system so that innovative activities were valued as highly as standard performance measures such as publications in peer-reviewed journals;[21] absent such a cultural change, workshop participants were somewhat pessimistic that innovative activity could be sufficiently encouraged and supported. In a similar vein, it was noted that a university's mission typically was to develop new knowledge and not to go about identifying new customers.

Developing Plans

Planning considerations play a number of prominent roles, including developing strategic implementation plans that relate goals to infrastructure and human resource issues; developing communications strategies; managing the time of key stakeholders to ensure that their time is not wasted; and planning for the ultimate institutionalization of the partnership or network so that its processes and benefits can be continued.

---

[19]On the other hand, the Bayh-Dole Act of 1980 (amended in 1986) enabled nonprofit institutions to receive patents on the results of publicly funded research and has been credited with the resulting significant expansion in universities' efforts to support patenting, licensing, and transfer to industrial firms of university research results, as well as providing incentives for university-industry partnerships. See Mowery (1998).

[20]There is a growing trend for industry to take IP not being commercialized, donate it to a university (as a tax write-off), and in some cases to lend researchers to help the university develop the technology even further and possibly commercialize it.

[21]A yearly luncheon recognizing faculty who have patent inventions was proposed as an example.

There also seemed to be broad agreement that the partnership should be treated as a business, which meant that the partnership should have a business model and plan.[22] According to workshop participants, these should provide potential investors and others with an idea of the potential value of the innovative activity, judged on the basis of the estimated size and identity of the customer base in the relevant market, the nature of competition and demand in the market,[23] and analysis demonstrating that the expected rewards justified the expected risks. The plan also should lay out the steps—and costs—involved in bringing the innovative product or process to market, including how resources are to be allocated to accomplish the partnership's goals.

Competing, Communicating, and Resolving Conflicts

When a partnership has addressed the foregoing issues, it is ready to compete, but the continued integrity and viability of the partnership can be challenged as a result of unforeseen developments and the changing motives of the partners. This requires continued communication among all partners and conflict resolution procedures.

Competing. Competing consists of bringing the innovative product or process to market in competition with other products or processes.

Communicating. Effective communication within the partnership is necessary, as is promotion of success outside the partnership. Community/stakeholder buy-in that supports the enterprise, including frequent meetings with stakeholders and other means for overcoming fragmentation and isolation, is needed to mobilize organizations and resources. Moreover, the "selling of success"—celebrating success stories—was viewed as crucial from the outset, and identifying and developing key audiences for marketing and public relations

---

[22]A typical conception of a business model is a one-page paper that describes how all of the elements of a business work together to build marketplace advantage and company value. The business model typically describes its intended customers and its marketing strategy for reaching them.

[23]The willingness of customers to pay for the innovation was specifically identified as being of interest.

was viewed as an instrumental means for drawing in additional resources. Since many principal investigators (PIs) lack expertise in effective public relations, some argued that a separate budgeting category needs to be created for public relations, and media contacts need to be included in the network.

Resolving Conflicts. As discussed above, participation in a partnership connoted an essential compatibility in the interests of universities and industry: The innovative capacity of universities could be harnessed to the proven technology of the private sector and made functional, manufacturable, and scaleable. However, as was described above, a number of potential areas of incompatibility were seen to offer the potential for university-industry friction, including differing time horizons and priorities, competing claims for royalties from intellectual property, and differences over the timing and scope for the dissemination of research results. In recognition of these— and other—potential flash points, workshop participants advocated a fairly sensible approach.

At the outset of a partnership, all partners should put their personal agendas on the table and ascertain the extent to which everyone's needs can be met. In some cases, areas of potential friction requiring tradeoffs may be creatively redirected into more productive arrangements. Rather than competing over shares of royalties, for example, universities might seek laboratory equipment or other in-kind investments, access to firm resources, consulting opportunities for faculty, or employment opportunities for students. Similarly, to the extent that universities are willing to modify performance and promotion criteria to weight patents and other evidence of innovative research as heavily as peer-reviewed publications are weighted, this can eliminate a source of potential friction that arises from the "publish or perish" reward system faced by most academic researchers and leads to a desire for speedy publication of results. Disputes that arise later in the partnership simply should be resolved with reference to what was described by one breakout session as a "hierarchy of values" that weighed the issue in contention against the benefits each party received from the partnership, the shared values of the partnership, and the interdependence of the partners.

CATALYZING ENABLING INFRASTRUCTURE TO FOSTER LONG-TERM INNOVATION

The PFI program also aims to catalyze the creation of the infrastructure that can sustain and nurture the spread of innovative activity over the long term. Workshop deliberations described infrastructure of three general kinds: that related to developing human capital, developing networks, and providing direct support for the innovation enterprise.

Developing Human Capital

To educate and train human capital for the research enterprise, workshop participants saw the requirement for an innovative educational process whose most important goal was serving the student. Such a program should be focused on creating an environment that rewards innovation and is characterized by passion and a commitment to success.

This process would identify talent as early as possible (from elementary school on), create good motivational teachers, and embrace versatility (e.g., affirmative action programs, recognition of cultural differences) to ensure that it was drawing upon the largest possible pool of new talent. As students progress, it is critical to make subjects real with hands-on education and training and to demonstrate the connections between popular programs and how they had progressed to that point. At the university level, the most important role of the university was seen as educating and training young scientists and engineers; good science and engineering students need to be recruited and then retained[24] and brought into partnerships with industry. And internships should work in both directions: faculty and student internships in industry and industry internships in universities.[25] Finally, young scientists and engineers need to serve as agents of change, i.e., by diffusing know-how and innovation.

---

[24]For a recent report on the subject, see National Science Foundation (1999).

[25]The NSF's Research Experiences for Undergraduates (REU) program, which provides a framework for internships with industry, was mentioned as a good model in this regard, as was the PFI program.

To accomplish this, workshop participants viewed as critical early participation from all stakeholders and buy-in from the top for the principle that the most important goal was serving students. And buy-in could be quite literal: It could require investment in additional plant and teachers for traditionally underserved populations; buy-outs of faculty time for sabbaticals, mentoring, and other activities; or monetary rewards for excellence in teaching or research.

The education and workforce challenges that were identified ranged from simply keeping students in the state to paying for program coordinators, facility space, equipment, etc., and reaching all stakeholders, especially minority-owned businesses. At a macro-level, there also are longer-term workforce challenges related to ensuring that the nation can develop (or attract and retain) needed science and technology (S&T) workers in key areas (see the box, below).[26]

Concern also was expressed about the challenges arising from adverse demographic trends, including an increasing ratio of pensioners to workers and chronic problems with the K–12 educational system.[27]

Creating Networks that Embed Social Capital

The intellectual capital and know-how embodied in young scientists and engineers, honed through advanced education and training, must be embedded in social networks characterized by shared commitment and trust. Such networks can be built only through extended interactions and problem-solving and represent a form of

---

[26]Future workforce challenges already have been recognized and are the subject of high-level attention. See National Science and Technology Council (2000). Additionally, the National Science Board currently has a task force that is examining national workforce policies for science and engineering. See National Science Foundation (2000), available at http://www.nsf.gov/nsb/documents/2000/nwp004/nwp004.htm. In considering the issue, however, one needs to consider the capacity of labor markets themselves to correct for increased demand by raising wages. See David and Hall (2000).

[27]See Good (2001). For an industry perspective on the challenges faced by the K–12 system and some suggested remedies, see Popper, Wagner, and Larson (1998), pp. 108–109. For a perspective on workforce issues, see National Research Council (1998), especially pp. 17–24, 46–47.

Ensuring an S&T Workforce for Future Areas of Innovation

According to a presentation from Mary Good[a], U.S. policymakers need to look at the implications of a U.S. S&T workforce that is both aging and changing in its composition. To illustrate why the United States should be concerned, she used the following example.

Many believe that the next generation of computing will be based on quantum computing, and Hewlett-Packard (HP), IBM, Lucent, and many universities accordingly have invested heavily in quantum computing research. Looking at members of the Quantum Science Research at HP's laboratories, however, two striking observations can be made. First, all of the U.S. members are over the age of 45; and second, all of the younger ones are non-U.S. citizens. This pattern also has been observed in the universities that are doing this type of research.

As Good pointed out, this is just one anecdote, in only one area of S&T, but it does raise several important policy-relevant questions. How can the United States reverse adverse trends that may be occurring in core areas of S&T and better ensure that the nation will have a future workforce with enough qualified workers in these areas? How can the nation draw enough U.S. students into the science and engineering workforce to ensure a robust indigenous capability in what appear to be emerging core areas of S&T? Failing that, how can the United States ensure the availability of H-1 visas and immigration-friendly policies for foreign students who are doing research in core S&T areas in U.S. universities and who might remain in the United States thereafter? If there are too few American students, and industry cannot hire foreign students, where will industry and universities find the expertise they need?

Although there are no simple answers to these questions, they are among those that the United States must consider and take action on to ensure the necessary intellectual capital to keep the United States competitive in the global market.

[a]Good (2001).

social capital that, in some workshop participants' minds, seemed to be the most important type of infrastructure of all.

As suggested by the earlier discussion of what is required to catalyze innovative partnerships, to create such networks requires a substantial investment of time and resources over an extended period of time. Although they may begin with a specific project in mind, such networks may grow and expand beyond the terms of the original partnership and yield additional relationships, projects, and partnerships.

The development of this sort of infrastructure is enhanced by leaders and organizations that undertake the full range of activities that can improve the prospects that researchers and business people with compatible interests simply can meet one another, and by a track record of successful partnerships that yield desired benefits to all participants and impel them to expand the network into other types of partnerships relevant to the engineering piece of the enterprise. It also is enhanced by successful marketing and public relations efforts that celebrate successes, thereby drawing other parties into the network, and in the dissemination of innovative practices that reflect learning curve phenomena.

Providing Physical Facilities and Support

A base of operational support is essential, and sustainability cannot exist without such operational support. The network therefore needs to provide this. Ultimately this was viewed as a resource issue—a diversified base of private investment providing support for all needed components. Among the components identified were:

- *An Incubator.* At the most basic level, innovation was seen to require a place that can facilitate routine exchanges between the business community and the university, where partners can meet and work.[28] This can be accomplished through a host of

---

[28]One study found R&D geographic spillover effects in France and concluded that "[t]his trend towards a proximate localisation can be explained by the complexity of the R&D process, which reflects the need to co-ordinate a set of heterogeneous competencies (combinatory complexity) and the intensity of technological changes (technological complexity)." See Carrincazeaux, Lung, and Rallet (2001). On the other

means, ranging from informal open door policies that stem from good university-industrial relations to formalized university-industry research centers. Whether formal or informal, such a location also can provide a venue for meetings, whether for partners or extension efforts to educate and build community.

- *Technical Support.* Beyond the faculty researchers and students who are doing the research and their industry partners, a range of issues requiring subject matter expertise are likely to be beyond the capabilities of the immediate partnership. Supporting infrastructure accordingly may include an office that provides in-house legal (e.g., patent assistance and IP policies), financial, marketing, and public relations expertise that can generate support from newspapers and business publications.

- *Management and Administrative Support.* Beyond the specialized expertise just described, a range of basic management and administrative functions—from managing personnel, payroll, and budgets to providing clerical, reception, and other services—need to be performed by competent, well-trained staff to enable the partners to focus on research and commercialization.

- *Laboratory Capacity and Other Physical Plants.* Needed infrastructure also can include various sorts of physical plants, including computers, lab equipment, machine tools, and laboratory or other working space.

- *Communications.* Infrastructure also needs to include support for a variety of alternative means of communication—LISTSERVs, websites, email aliases, moderated email discussions, mailings, and other means—both among the partners and between partners and other stakeholders.[29] This may include capabilities to make videos and CD-ROMs to assist marketing efforts.

---

hand, Love and Roper provide a skeptical view of the importance of location and network effects on the success of innovation for manufacturing plants in three other European countries. See Love and Roper (2001).

[29]For example, participants mentioned a website, mainscience.org, which includes proposals and abstracts on research from researchers and reaches 3,000 people a week.

- *Reliable Sources of Capital.* Finally, needed infrastructure includes venture capital firms, angel investors, commercial banks, government, foundations, and other sources (e.g., Small Business Innovative Research (SBIR) grants) that can provide start-up, bridge, or other funding.

Beyond the fundamental elements of needed infrastructure just described, some argued that the PFI also needs to attend to a core constituency—members of Congress. Given that the federal government's role in promoting innovation is a politically controversial topic on Capitol Hill, it is necessary to ensure that elected leaders understand and support the PFI program's aims, that the program address elected leaders' potential concerns, and that there are no disconnects between project and program metrics and the political view of the program's goals. According to some, a tight linkage between project and program goals and metrics and a broader communication strategy were needed for the PFI. This strategy should include conversations with congressional representatives regarding what they expect out of this program and what metrics are appropriate (or inappropriate) for evaluating the program.

Challenges and Barriers to Sustainability

Workshop participants identified a number of key challenges or barriers to the emergence of these characteristics. These include turf battles among stakeholders; burn out; clashes with university culture reflected in institutional reward systems and rigid policies regarding intellectual property, startups, private sector engagement, and other matters; maintaining an ability to learn from other participants; having the right people in the right place at the right time; and the vagaries of politics.

Measurement Issues

Outcome Measures: Capacity. Another difficult-to-measure outcome was the marginal increase in aggregate capacity that had resulted from the PFI program. At the project level, this was discussed in three different forms. First, increased capacity was discussed in terms of the actual infrastructure (laboratory equipment, facilities, etc.) that had been added as a result of the partnership. Second, it was discussed in terms of the value added to individual partners' infrastructure that arose from exploiting the partnership's synergies. Third was training and workforce development, discussed largely in terms of providing research professors with opportunities to apply know-how to commercial problems and opportunities for graduate students to develop know-how regarding technology application and entrepreneurship.

Capacity that had been built as a result of the PFI program—whether in terms of infrastructure or of training and workforce development—was seen as a summative outcome at the program level; to the extent that the measurement problems could be resolved at the project level, however, it generally appeared to be a simple matter of aggregation for the program as a whole.

Outcome Measures: Sustainability. Although their measurement was not discussed in much detail, a number of suggested outcomes were identified as being of interest for assessing the sustainability of the partnerships. These included outcomes related to the survival and self-perpetuation of the partnership; project staff in the community; success at fund-raising activities; cross-membership on boards and other organizations; the growth of the partnership (i.e., its ability to attract new people and organizations to join the partnership); partnering for other grants and continuation even after a lack of success in receiving these grants; and the emergence of new innovation-oriented partnerships.

For a host of reasons, assessing the sustainability of each partnership was seen as a challenging enterprise. First, there was some concern that the short (two to three year) time horizon for PFI grants probably was too short a window for assessing sustainability; the sustainability of a partnership might not be known until five or even 10 years after its creation. Accordingly, workshop participants wanted to know how those involved in the partnership turned out five years later—whether they stayed in the game and pursued this sort of activity well after the grant ended.

Another reason for the difficulty was that a focus on the sustainability of the partnership might obscure the importance of the larger goal of catalyzing innovation; in this view, it was the quality of the innovation that mattered, not whether a partnership survived at some nominal level.[30] This point recognized the transitivity and "creative destruction" that are inherent in the innovation enterprise: A partnership that makes sense for today's innovative project may not make sense for tomorrow's. But it also pointed to the potential importance of partnerships evolving into broader networks that might link compatible partners who can choose to combine and recombine in different ways.[31] This latter view of partnerships—as seeds that have the potential for evolving and growing into a broader network that could itself catalyze additional partnerships and innovative activity—was one that seemed to be widely, if only tacitly, embraced by workshop participants, and one that was not explored in much detail in the workshop.[32]

Sustainability of the partnerships across the entire PFI program also was a summative outcome measure: To the extent that the difficulties in measuring the sustainability of individual projects could be resolved at the project level, it was a simple matter of indicating the number or proportion of projects that were judged as sustainable.

Signposts. Also suggested were measures that addressed a number of issues related to the partnerships themselves, including:

•   *Organizational Issues.* How was the partnership formed? Is the leadership team in place? Is the leadership structure of the partnership settled? Can it be easily described to others so that they understand how the partnership is organized and how it works? Are the necessary administrative arrangements in place (e.g., budget, IP, support staff)? Are information infrastructure, personnel, other resources "integrated" in the operation of the partnership (integration needs to be measured)? Are policies and rules sufficiently flexible?

---

[30]One breakout session asked how one compared a partnership that survived but did not succeed at generating an innovation with one that was successful in innovating but where the partnership dissolved.

[31]On innovation networks, see Freeman (1991).

[32]The evaluation of sustainability would need to take into account the intended life of the partnership, whether it is a short-term project, which, when its objective is achieved, is dissolved or whether it a longer-term relationship that is being established. Evaluating sustainability should be based on when the goals are to be achieved.

- *Agreements.* Have the necessary agreements on benefits, burden-sharing, and other issues (e.g., regarding intellectual property) been negotiated? What have members of the partnership agreed to share? Dollars? Risk? Resources? Graduate students? Professors? Measures are needed to look at the quality of relationship. How long did it take to come to an agreement?

- *Finances.* Have start-up funding needs been identified? Have sources of support been identified, including internal resources (including, e.g., "skunk works"), grant funding (federal, state, local), philanthropy, private sector (angels, venture capital, corporate)? Have sales and other revenue sources been identified? Are budgets and finances transparent and able to be tracked? Is there flexibility in moving funds? Have processes been established for managing in-kind and matching funding and for linking in-kind support to hard cash?

- *Plans.* Is there a project plan? Is there a business plan that assesses the market and the demand for the innovation? Have potential testing/beta sites been identified in the business plan? Is there a financial plan? Is there agreement regarding the processes for modification of these plans? Do the plans reflect reasonable expectations? Is there a risk analysis scheme?

- *Communications.* Are the partners actively engaged? Does the partnership hold regular meetings? Is there a process for communication? Are partners communicating well? Are there provisions for talking to top management to resolve problems? Have measures for outreach activities been established? Does the partnership produce products for dissemination?

- *Diversity.* What level of participation is there from traditionally underserved populations and institutions?

Workshop participants seemed somewhat divided on these measures, however. On the one hand, there was an interest in understanding the partnerships themselves in ways that could generate the information that can help participants in their activities and help the NSF in further refining the PFI program. On the other hand, there also was a clear recognition that successfully encouraging participants to keep good records cannot only be difficult but it can divert their focus from innovative activities to administrative and documentary ones. The solution for some was to be found not in large and complex survey instruments but in identifying a few "nuggets" that needed to be reported to track the progress of the partnerships, for identifying best practices, etc.

BROADENING PARTICIPATION IN THE NATIONAL INNOVATION ENTERPRISE

A final aim of the PFI program is to broaden the participation of underrepresented, disadvantaged, or underserved individuals and institutions. Workshop participants discussed this issue almost entirely in terms of specific means for measuring project- and program-level success at promoting this aim. Accordingly, we turn directly to the issue of measurement.

Measurement Issues

Outcome Measures. At the level of the individual, the PFI program aims to expand opportunities for students and professors who are women, minorities, and members of other demographic groups; at the level of the community and region, it aims to encourage new bases for economic and workforce development in less well-endowed locales; and at the institutional level, the PFI program aims to catalyze innovation in smaller institutions and in those that do not have extensive experience performing government-supported research.

At the project level, participants suggested that individual partnerships should report what types of people were involved in the partnership and provide basic demographic information related to gender, race and ethnicity, and other factors.

At the program level, achievement of diversity goals can be aggregated up from project-level data, e.g., indicating the number of minority, female, or other individuals who participated in all of the PFI programs.

Signposts. The signposts were essentially identical to the outcome measures.

CONCLUSIONS

There was broad support in the workshop for a number of propositions regarding partnerships and networks. First, most seemed to believe that the NSF should foster technology and economic development through local networks and support alternative models of partnerships, clusters, and networks for encouraging innovation. There also seemed to be a shared view that the PFI's (and NSF's) support for innovation should not amount to an entitlement. The aim, consistent with the PFI's program goals, should be to catalyze innovation by bootstrapping innovative partnerships and networks and providing the necessary resources and technical assistance to improve the chances that they could become self-sustaining. It was recognized, however, that some partnerships would achieve sustainability and others would not.[33]

Although universities were seen to have a major role to play in innovative partnerships, there was broad support for the proposition that cultural changes are needed to secure that role and to ensure balance between educational, research, and innovation goals. A recurring complaint was that university policies and promotion and other reward systems too often fail to encourage—or even actively discourage—efforts to apply and commercialize research. Many workshop participants argued that this needed to change, even as they recognized the risks to educational and academic research missions of becoming overly focused on commercialization of new knowledge.

---

[33]One reviewer of this report suggested that sustainability is not and does not always have to be a goal in partnerships. Indeed, the world is full of fluid organizational arrangements to drive the innovation process. However, in the case of PFI, sustainability is an important factor.

Chapter Five

IMPLICATIONS FOR THE NSF

In this final chapter, we summarize the main conclusions of the workshop regarding the evaluation of the PFI program and identify major issues related to the NSF's role in the innovation process. We close with our own observations regarding the sorts of questions that the NSF should seek to address as it adapts itself to the changing needs of the nation in the new century.

EVALUATING THE PFI PROGRAM

Chapters Three and Four identified a large number of suggested measures related to various issues attendant to innovation and partnerships. We now step back from these details to summarize the arguments related to the broader question of evaluating the PFI program.

There was nearly unanimous support for a formal evaluation of the PFI program by an independent, paid evaluator. Such an effort was viewed as being consistent both with the NSF's general commitment to evaluation as an aid to outcome-based management and with its specific obligations under the Government Performance and Results Act of 1993 (GPRA).[1]

According to participants, such an evaluation should rely on objective measures that can lead to insights regarding the most critical questions related to innovation and the partnerships themselves. It

---

[1]The text of the act may be found at http://www.nsf.gov/od/gpra/law.htm.

also should provide outcome and process measures (or, as used in this report, signposts) both for individual projects and for the program as a whole.[2] Although PIs should be consulted in the development of evaluation metrics—and should assist in identifying which are appropriate for their partnership—an outside evaluator was viewed as necessary to ensure objectivity and impartiality in the evaluation.

As described above, an evaluation of the PFI program also should leverage off lessons learned and best practices from the many other NSF programs that promote innovation and link universities and industry. Moreover, many argued that the NSF should use the opportunity of an evaluation to turn the lens back on itself: To inform further refinements of the PFI program, the evaluation should include measures of the quality of the technical and other assistance the NSF is providing to PFI partnerships, the extent to which that support helped the partnerships, and what other assistance also might be made available.

Although some seemed to imply that there was something of a sense of urgency on the matter of an evaluation—e.g., that data that would be needed for an evaluation might not be collected or might become lost—others seemed to argue that since actual outcomes could not be known for several years at the very earliest, this was not a particularly urgent matter. In either case, however, the basic need for a proper evaluation of the PFI program was generally accepted.

THE NSF'S ROLES IN INNOVATION

As described in the preceding chapters, beyond its traditional roles of promoting the public good by supporting research and education, the NSF was seen by participants to have a number of critical roles, including catalyzing change, forging connections, enhancing institutions, establishing standards and identifying best practices, enhancing diversity, and nurturing alternative models. Each will be summarized next.

---

[2]See Appendix G, which summarizes workshop discussions regarding both some design principles and the potential challenges in such an evaluation.

Catalyzing Change

The NSF has a unique ability to lead in catalyzing needed institutional changes in the university. This can be accomplished by providing an NSF stamp of approval for university researchers working with industry and developing ranking criteria, awards and other reward systems, and other incentives that can foster needed cultural changes in universities and lead to greater university support for the application of research.

Enhancing Institutions

One means for catalyzing change is creating incentives for the development of institutional capacity for innovation. This can include seeding the creation of multidisciplinary or industry-oriented university-based centers of excellence and assisting existing centers in fostering capacity to meet industry needs.

Forging Connections

The NSF has an important role to play in improving the performance of the information markets that make innovation possible. This can be accomplished by sponsoring meetings and other mechanisms that heighten the prospects that interested and potentially complementary parties will become aware of one another, supporting the development of networks of various kinds (e.g., alliances, LISTSERVs with threaded discussions), and other means.

Establishing Standards and Identifying Best Practices

The NSF also can serve as an honest broker in developing relevant standards and metrics, identifying lessons learned and best practices, and ensuring their widest possible dissemination. Leadership in the development of appropriate standards and metrics is needed—particularly for some of the harder-to-measure aspects of innovation and partnerships—since it is generally beyond the capacity of individual partnerships to establish a consistent framework themselves.[3] The NSF's diverse portfolio of programs that focus on innovation and fostering university-industry linkages also gives it a unique capacity to compile and disseminate lessons learned and best practices from these many programs, both among principal investigators and among broader constituencies.[4] The NSF also can sponsor conferences of awardees who meet more regularly to share insights, as well as supporting other means of enhancing communication and learning.

Nurturing Alternative Models

An apparent consensus in the workshop was that innovation functionally required sufficiently frequent and routine interactions between researchers and industry to develop the necessary levels of mutual understanding and trust that could lead to fruitful partnerships. This in turn required stable infrastructure that could provide both a reliable place for these interactions and operational support.

Less explicitly, it was clear from the workshop that participants believed that a range of alternative models was available for incubating and otherwise supporting innovative partnerships, networks, and other arrangements and that each of these alternative models deserves support: S&T parks and campuses, incubators and accelerators, centers of excellence, ERCs and I/UCRCs, and other settings (see the box, below).

Indeed, workshop participants seemed to endorse both an expansion in the NSF's support for innovation and partnerships through the PFI and continued efforts by the NSF to further diversify its programmatic support for innovation. The presentations and workshop discussions evidenced substantial enthusiasm for the PFI program and other NSF programs that support innovation and university-industry collaborative efforts, without favoring any particular model (e.g., PFI) over any other (e.g., I/UCRCs).[5]

---

[3]For additional reading, see Norling (1997).

[4]For example, some suggested that the NSF might arrange for speakers from the I/UCRC program, and their evaluators, to provide their insights on evaluation.

[5]It is worth pointing out that a number of workshop attendees were neither grantees nor had any intention of applying for a PFI grant.

An Infrastructure Model for Innovation

There is a range of models available for supporting innovative partnerships, networks, and other arrangements. Marye Anne Fox[a] described one such model being used at North Carolina State University.

NC State's Centennial Campus provides physical infrastructure that allows members of academe and industry to come together for the integration of industry activities into academic programs, and brings together workforce, ideas, new approaches to education, and technology transfer on a single campus. Centennial Campus is a carefully planned community designed to foster innovation and support a unique culture of partnerships that bring ideas, people, and technology together in new ways. It is unique in comparison to other types of research parks, in that it looks for partnerships; ways for industry or government partners to enhance university academic and educational programs while concurrently bringing value to what they do.

The goals of the Centennial Campus have been to break down some of the disciplinary structures that have been developed at the university over the last few years, and also to expand the results to industry. The campus plan centers around its R&D neighborhoods, which are each dedicated to a subject area and house one or more related core university programs. Buildings with space for R&D facilities are available for select businesses and government agencies whose operations relate to these program areas. The million square feet of physical space on the campus has been generated by investments from the state, private sector, and from government. On campus, there are 53 companies (16 large, 10 small, and 27 startups), seven government agencies, seven nonprofit companies, and 23 R&D centers, primarily funded by the state. 900 employees from the private sector, 900 faculty, staff and post-docs, and 1,400 students are involved in the Campus. Creation of this technology infrastructure permits NC State's students to make non-traditional connections with industry and government.

The Centennial Campus is just one model available for supporting and sustaining innovation. Other models include traditional S&T parks and campuses; incubators and accelerators; centers of excellence; ERCs and I/UCRCs; and other settings.

[a]Fox (2001).

The workshop devoted less attention to the topic of selection criteria and the difficulties of identifying for support only those enterprises that would not ordinarily be supported by industry.[6]

LOOKING TO THE FUTURE

In closing, we now shift from one role—faithful reporters of the workshop proceedings—to another—policy analysts and advisors to the NSF and the PFI program.

As the NSF takes stock of its past experience and reflects on how it will express its future commitment to catalyzing innovation, we believe that it should ask itself a number of questions, strategic in nature, to illuminate the benefits and costs associated with different paths. Among these are the following:

- Which of the available programs and models for promoting innovation is the most appropriate tool for the NSF to use under which circumstances?

- How can the NSF refine its understanding of the relative effectiveness of its innovation programs in promoting its objectives?

- In what ways can the NSF exploit synergies between programs (e.g., PFI programs that are incubated in an ERC or I/UCRC)?

- In what ways can (or should) this mosaic of programs and models be considered together as a larger whole to ensure that the NSF's enterprise-wide portfolio of innovation-catalyzing programs matches its strategic intent and its presumed desire to achieve an optimal program mix and level of diversification?

- What is the best balance or tradeoff among the various potentially conflicting imperatives (e.g., education and workforce development, academic research, innovation, and diversity)?

---

[6]For example, one would want to make sure that the NSF funds do not "crowd out" private funding. On this issue, see Wallsten (2000), and David and Hall, (2000).

- What factors are associated with the success or failure of technology partnerships, networks, and clusters?[7]

Insofar as these questions seems to be at the heart of the NSF's effort to build a new foundation for innovation while remaining true to its purpose, they seem particularly deserving of further analysis, discussion, and debate.

---

[7]On technology clusters, see, for example, Porter (1990), Sternberg (1990), Saxenian (1996), BankBoston Economics Department (1997), Malecki (1997), Luger (1999), and Schmandt (1999).

PFI STEERING GROUP MEMBERS

Table A.1

Workshop Steering Committee

Name	Institution
William Sibley[a]	Oklahoma Center for the Advancement of Science and Technology
Hans Brisch	State Higher Education Executive Officers Association
Arturo Bronson	University of Texas at El Paso
Don Cotten	University of Southern Mississippi
Kerry Davidson	Louisiana Board of Regents
Larry Farrar	Montec Research
Jim Lovelace	University of Maryland
Charles Moreland	North Carolina State University
Walter Plosila	Battelle Memorial Institute
Ann Redelfs	University of California, San Diego

[a]Chairman.

PFI GRANTEES

Table B.1

FY 2001 Partnership for Innovation Grantees

Institution (State)	Project
Arizona State University (AZ)	AzPATH—A Partnership for Housing Innovation in Arizona
California Institute of Technology	Entrepreneurial Fellows Program
Fisk University (TN)	Room temperature infrared lasers based on rare earth doped $CaGa_2Se_4$
Ilisagvik College (AK)	Distance Education Delivery for Isolated Rural Communities: A Contingency Approach
Indiana University/Purdue University—Indianapolis (IN)	Partnerships for Innovation: A Center of Excellence in Regenerative Biology
Morgan State University (MD)	Maryland Technology Partnership for Innovation
North Carolina A&T State University (NC)	Low Cost Resin Transfer Molded Based Carbon/Carbon Composites for Automotive to Space Applications
Pennsylvania State University (PA)	A Partnership for Innovation: Promoting Education and Research in Nanofabrication Applications to Biology and Medicine
Rochester Institute of Technology (NY)	Upstate Alliance for Innovation
Rutgers University New Brunswick (NJ)	Models for Better Academic-Industrial Partnerships to Create Value from Concepts
South Dakota State University (SD)	Great Plains Rapid Prototyping Consortium
Tennessee Technological University (TN)	Expanding Innovation Opportunities in Tennessee
Texas A&M University (TX)	Synergistic Electronic Commerce (SynreCom) Partnership for Innovation
Tuskegee University (AL)	A Partnership for Innovations in Nancomposites Technology

Table B.1 (continued)

Institution (State)	Project
University of Arkansas (AR)	Innovation Incubator: Flaming the Sparks of Creativity
University of Central Oklahoma (OK)	Institute for Emerging Technologies: Strategic Technology Education for Non-Tech Majors
University of Idaho (ID)	Farm and Ornamental Fish
University of Massachusetts-Amherst (MA)	Innovation Networks: A Strategy of the Regional Technology Alliance
University of Missouri-Kansas City (MO)	The Kansas City Regional Innovation Alliance
University of North Carolina System (NC)	North Carolina Technology Development Initiative: A Novel Approach to Assess, Disseminate and Test a University/Venture Capital/Incubator Partnership Model
University of Puerto Rico (PR)	Partnership for Innovation to Enhance Puerto Rico's Economic Development
University of Texas—Pan American (TX)	Rapid Product Development in International Production
Virginia Polytechnic Institute and State University (VA)	Advanced Materials for PEM-based Fuel Cell Systems
West Virginia University (WV)	Advanced Polymer Materials for Construction and Aquaculture Marketing Development

SOURCE: National Science Foundation Partnerships for Innovation program.

PFI WORKSHOP ATTENDEES

Table C.1

PFI Workshop Attendees

Daniel Akins, City College of New York

Jeff Alexander, Washington CORE LLC

Stuart Arnett, New Hampshire Division of Economic Development

Phyllis Arnette, Texas Instruments Incorporated

Richard Ash, Mentor Technology Ventures LLC

Philip Auerswald, Harvard University

Marietta Baba, Wayne State University

Gary Bachula, Internet2

Diola Bagayoko, Southern University and A&M College

Allen Baker, Vital Strategies

Anita Balachandra, Maryland Technology Development Corporation

Ramesh Bapat, RAND

Howard Bashford[a], Arizona State University

Richard Bendis, Kansas Technology Enterprise Corporation

David Benfield, South Dakota State University

William Bernard, TCE

Joseph Bordogna, National Science Foundation

Donald Boyd[a], University of Rochester

Karen Boykin, University of Alabama

Irene Brahmakulam, RAND

Ernest Brannon, University of Idaho

Michael Breton[a], Rutgers University

LeeRoy Bronner[a], Morgan State University

Arturo Bronson, University of Texas at El Paso

Arnold Burger[a], Fisk University

Chris Busch, University of Wyoming Research Office

Frederick Byron, Jr.[a], University of Massachusetts

Elias Carayannis, The George Washington University

Michael Champness, Business-Higher Education Forum

Jaymie Chernoff[a], University of Massachusetts

Mark Coburn[a], University of Rochester

Julie Cole, Wake Forest University

Ron Cooper, Center for Excellence in IT & Telecommunications, Oklahoma State University

Donald Cotton, University of Southern Mississippi

Ronald Crawford, University of Idaho

Gerard Crawley, University of South Carolina

Kenneth Currie[a], Tennessee Technological University

George Daddis, Jr.[a], InScitek Microsystems, Inc.

Julio Davalos[a], West Virginia University

Kerry Davidson, Louisiana Board of Regents

Isadore Davis, Raytheon Defense Systems

Laura DeNinno, IT Cluster/Information Technology Association of Southern Arizona

Jere Denton, CEO Focus, LLC

Lee Eiden, U.S. Department of Education

Barbara Evans, Lousiana Partnership for Technology and Innovation

Larry Farrar, Montec Research

Stephen Fonash[a], Pennsylvania State University

Mary Anne Fox, North Carolina State University

Kevin Franklin, University of California, San Diego

William Gardiner, Prince George's Economic Development Corporation

Preston Gilbert, Syracuse University

Kinsey Gimbel, QRC Division of Macro International, Inc.

Manuel Gomez[a], University of Puerto Rico

Miguel Gonzalez[a], University of Texas-Pan American

Mary Good, University of Arkansas, Little Rock

James Gosz, New Mexico EPSCoR, University of New Mexico

James Green[a], Cumberland Emerging Technologies

Margaret Grucza, Industrial Research Institute

Joseph Hammang, Rhode Island Economic Policy Council

Marion Harmon, Florida A&M University

David Harris[a], University of Central Oklahoma

Steve Hart, Interpretech, LLC

Charles Hatch[a], University of Idaho

Robert Heard, National Association of Seed and Venture Funds

Christopher Hill, George Mason University

Chris Hollinsed, DuPont Central Research and Development

Gary Holloway[a], Evendale Bearings, Seals, and Drives

Kent Hughes, Woodrow Wilson International Center for Scholars

John Hurt, National Science Foundation

Brian Jackson, RAND

Shaik Jeelani, Tuskegee University

Glen Johnson[a], Tennessee Technological University

James Kadtke, RAND

Maryellen Kelley, Pamet Hill Associates

Barbara Kimbell, University of New Mexico

Taffy Kingscott, IBM Corporation

Joachim Kohn[a], Rutgers University

Fae Korsmo, National Science Foundation

Rajiv Kulkarni, Department of Community and Economic Development

Edward Lane, North Carolina Center for Entrepreneurship and Technology

Eric Larson, RAND

Gina Lee Glauser, Syracuse University

Dennis Leyden, University of North Carolina at Greensboro

Julio Lopez-Ferrao, National Science Foundation

Mark Luker, EDUCAUSE

Ronald MacQuarrie[a], University of Missouri-Kansas City

Hassan Mahfuz[a], Tuskegee University

Reza Maleki[a] , South Dakota State University

Michael Marcantel, Louisiana Partnership for Technology and Innovation

Carol McConica, Oregon State University

Chris McGahey, RAND

James McGrath[a], Virginia Tech

Mark McLellan. Texas A&M University

Bruce McWilliams, The George Washington University

Gary Meaney[a], Texas Engineering Extension Service

Roberta Melton, Prince George's County Economic Development Corporation

Garrett Menning, American Association for the Advancement of Science/U.S. Agency for International Development

Egils Milbergs, the National Coalition for Advanced Manufacturing

Charles Moreland, North Carolina State University

Mark Morgan, QRC Division of Macro International Inc.

Francisco Moris, National Science Foundation

J. Ted Morris[a], North Carolina Technological Development Authority

Kazue Muroi, Washington CORE

John Naleway, Marker Gene Technologies, Inc.

E. Roger Novak, Jr., Novak Biddle Venture Partners

Athar Osama, RAND

Lori Perine, Interpretech, LLC

Thomas Persons, Sr., the South Carolina Technology Alliance

Cynthia Phillips, Decision Catalyst, Inc.

Walter Plosila, Battelle Memorial Institute

Jerry Plunkett[a], Kansas Structural Composites, Inc.

Steven Popper, RAND

David Pramer, Rutgers, the State University of New Jersey

Earnestine Psalmonds, North Carolina A&T State University

David Radzanowski, Office of Management and Budget

Guillermo Ramirez, University of Kansas

Ann Redelfs, University of California, San Diego

George Reeder[a], TVR Communications

Victor Rivera[a], University of Puerto Rico

Karen Roberts, Greater Washington Board of Trade

J. David Roessner, SRI International

Salvatore Romano[a], New Jersey Center for Biomaterials

Sally Rood, Federal Laboratory Consortium

RoseAnn Rosenthal, Ben Franklin Technology Partners

Renee Rottner[a], California Institute of Technology

Joel Russ, Maine Science and Technology Foundation

Greg Salamo[a], University of Arkansas

Jerome Schaufeld[a], Mass Ventures Corporation

Abraham Schwartz[a], Center for Quantitative Cytometry

Randy Schwartz, North Dakota Department of Economic Development and Finance

Stanley Scott[a], Ilisagvik College

Gary Sera[a], Texas Engineering Extension Service

Kunigal Shivakumar[a], North Carolina A&T State University

William Sibley, Oklahoma Center for the Advancement of Science and Technology

Phillip Singerman[a], Maryland Technology Development Corporation

Oliver Smith, Phillips Alaska, Inc.

Richard Spivack, Department of
Commerce
Beth Starbuck, Calyx, Inc
Martha Stewart, University of Alaska
David Stocum[a], Indiana University-
Purdue University Indianapolis
Jerry Straalsund, Spokane
Intercollegiate Research and
Technology Institute
Gregory Tassey, Department of
Commerce
Jonathon Tucker, George Mason
University
Mel Ustad, University of South
Dakota
Daniel Van Belleghem, National
Computational Science Alliance
Access
Frances Van Scoy, West Virgina
Experimental Program to Stimulate
Competitive Research, West
Virginia University

Krishna Vedula, University of
Massachusetts-Lowell
Michael von Spakovsky[a], Virginia
Tech
Nicholas Vonortas, George
Washington University
Caroline Wagner, RAND
Michelle Waites[a], Phillips Community
College of University of Arkansas
Deborah Watts, Technology
Development Group
David Winwood[a], North Carolina
State University
Lisa Wyatt Knowlton, Third Sector
Strategies, LLC
Marjorie Zack[a], University of
Rochester
David Zuckerman[a], Art Center
College of Design

[a]PFI grantee.

PFI WORKSHOP AGENDA

JUNE 18, 2001

8:25   Welcome

  — Steven Popper, Senior Economist, RAND

8:30   Opening Remarks

  —Joseph Bordogna, Deputy Director, National Science Foundation

8:50   Overview of the Partnerships for Innovation (PFI) Program

  —John Hurt, Program Director, PFI, National Science Foundation, and Mariann (Sam) Jelinek, Program Director, Innovation and Organizational Change, National Science Foundation

9:15   An Industry Perspective on Partnerships

  —Egils Milbergs, President, National Coalition for Advanced Manufacturing

9:45   A University Perspective on Partnerships

  —Marye Anne Fox, Chancellor, North Carolina State University

10:15   Break

10:30   Panel Discussion: Partnerships, Clusters, and Networks

—Moderator: J. David Roessner, Associate Director, Science and Technology Program, SRI International

1.   Local and Regional View—Richard Bendis, President, KTEC

2.   National View—Kathleen (Taffy) Kingscott, Director, Public Affairs, IBM

3.   International View—Mary Good, Dean, Donaghey College of Information and Systems Engineering, University of Arkansas, Little Rock

11:30   Question-and-Answer Session

12:00   Lunch

—The Importance of Sustainability and Ways to Achieve It, Kent Hughes, Public Policy Scholar, Woodrow Wilson International Center for Scholars

1:15   Breakout Sessions—two sessions each per topic:

1.   From Research to Commercialization (1)

Resource: Gary Holloway, Evendale Bearings, Seals and Drives; Kunigal Shivakumar, North Carolina A&T State University

Facilitator: Larry Farrar, Montec Research

2.   From Research to Commercialization (2)

Resource: Frederick Byron, Jr., and Jaymie Chernoff, University of Massachusetts Amherst; Jerome Schaufeld, Mass Ventures Corporation

Facilitator: Don Cotten, University of Southern Mississippi

3.   Infrastructure Development for Research and Commercialization (1)

Resource: Ken Currie, Tennessee Technological University; James   Green, Cumberland Emerging Technologies

Facilitator: William Sibley, Oklahoma Center for the Advancement of Science and Technology

4.   Infrastructure Development for Research and Commercialization (2)

Resource: David Winwood, University of North Carolina; J. Ted Morris, NC Technological Development Authority, Inc.

Facilitator: Charles Moreland, North Carolina State University

5.   Workforce Development and Enhancement (1)

Resource: Stephen Fonash, Pennsylvania State University

Facilitator: John Hurt, National Science Foundation

6.   Workforce Development and Enhancement (2)

Resource: David Harris, University of Central Oklahoma; George Reeder, TVR Communications

Facilitator: Ann Redelfs, University of California, San Diego

7.   Intellectual Property Concerns and Barriers (1)[1]

Resource: Manuel Gomez, University of Puerto Rico; Victor Rivera, University of Puerto Rico; Abe Schwartz, Caribbean MicroParticles Corporation

Facilitator: Brian Jackson, RAND

---

[1]Consolidated into a single session.

8.   Intellectual Property Concerns and Barriers (2)[2]

Resource: Joachim Kohn, Rutgers University; Salvatore Romano, New Jersey Center for Biomaterials

Facilitator: Bruce McWilliams, The George Washington University

3:30   Break

3:45   Reports from Breakout Sessions

5:00   Partnerships for Innovation Awardees Poster Session/Social

JUNE 19, 2001

8:00   Venture Capital for Partnerships

—E. Roger Novak, Jr., Founding Partner, Novak Biddle VenturePartners

8:30   Assessment and Performance Measures

—Maryellen Kelley, Partner, Pamet Hill Associates

9:00   Breakout Sessions—two sessions per topic:

1.   Sustainability (1)

Resource: Isadore Davis, Raytheon Defense Systems; Laura DeNinno, IT Cluster/ITASA

Facilitator: Kerry Davidson, Louisiana Board of Regents

2.   Sustainability (2)

Resource: Donald Boyd, Mark Coburn, and Marjorie Zack, University of Rochester; George Daddis, InSciTek Microsystems, Inc.

---

[2]Consolidated into a single session.

Facilitator: Walter Plosila, Battelle Memorial Institute

3.   Metrics/Evaluation/Assessment (1)

Resource: Mark Morgan, QRC Division of Macro International, Inc.

Facilitator: Julio Lopez-Ferrao, National Science Foundation

4.   Metrics/Evaluation/Assessment (2)

Resource: Christopher Hill, George Mason University

Facilitator: Jonathon Tucker, George Mason University

5.   Management and Financial Planning (1)

Resource: LeeRoy Bronner, Morgan State University; Philip Singerman, Maryland Technology Development Corporation

Facilitator: Arturo Bronson, University of Texas at El Paso

6.   Management and Financial Planning (2)

Resource: Robert Heard, National Association of Seed and Venture Funds

Facilitator: Philip Auerswald, Harvard University

11:15   Break

11:30   Reports from Breakout Sessions

12:15   Wrap-Up and Concluding Remarks: John Hurt, National Science Foundation

CHARGES TO BREAKOUT SESSIONS

This appendix documents the questions each breakout session was charged with addressing.

JUNE 18 SESSIONS

From Research to Commercialization

- What are the main characteristics of commercially useful research?
- What are the most efficient ways for the academic sector to target firms that might want to partner with them and can provide the needed resources?
- What are the most efficient ways for firms to find academic partners?
- What are the principal challenges or barriers to commercialization?
- What are the best means for eliminating them or reducing their effect?
- What roles can the NSF play in the commercialization process?

Infrastructure Development for Research and Commercialization

- What are the principal types of infrastructure needed

— To foster the commercialization of research?

— To communicate to potential users the goals of research, its relevance to their commercial products and processes?

— To disseminate research results to potential users?

— To scale up to commercial application (e.g., financial capital, learning curves)?

— To fully exploit the value of patents and other IP?

- What roles can the NSF play in fostering the development of needed infrastructure?

Workforce Development and Enhancement

- What are the principal types of infrastructure needed

  — To foster workforce development and enhancement?

  — To educate and train human capital for the research enterprise?

  — To educate and train the workforce?

- How, if at all, does the NSF need to change or improve upon its role in workforce development and enhancement?

Intellectual Property Concerns and Barriers

- What types of benefits (e.g., revenues from licensing and patents, sponsored research, internships for students, funding for equipment) can researchers derive from their IP?

- What are the principal IP issues that need to be successfully resolved by each of the partnerships?

  — From the university perspective

  — From the industry perspective

- What are the main challenges or barriers to their resolution?

- What are the best means for resolving disagreement?

- What if any roles can the NSF play in assisting in resolving IP concerns and barriers?

JUNE 19 SESSIONS

Sustainability

- What are likely to be the key characteristics of sustainable partnerships?
- What means are available for developing these characteristics?
- What are the key challenges or barriers to their emergence and how can they be overcome?
- What if any roles can the NSF play in reducing or eliminating these challenges and barriers?

Metrics/Evaluation/Assessment

- What process measures should be used to evaluate progress before actual outcomes emerge from each partnership?
- What outcome measures should be used to evaluate results at the end of each partnership?
- What other performance measures should be used in assessing the partnerships?

Management and Financial Planning

- What are the key characteristics of a successfully managed partnership?
- What are the main challenges or barriers to successful management and what means are available for overcoming them?
- What are the key elements of a good financial plan?
- What are the main challenges or barriers to financial planning and what means are available for overcoming them?
- What roles can the NSF play that would be both useful and appropriate?

SUMMARY OF KEY WORKSHOP FINDINGS AND RECOMMENDATIONS

The NSF has developed a set of goals to complement its overall vision: (1) people, (2), ideas, and (3) tools. Most of the comments and recommendations from the breakout sessions have been categorized in Table F.1 under these three main headings. The remaining points were categorized under sustainability, which transcends and pertains to these three headings.

Workshop participants identified two main areas of focus within the people category: current and future workforce, in general, and those specifically involved in partnerships. Participants also recognized ideas leading to new knowledge power innovation and productivity in today's economy. Ideas must be communicated and shared between university and industry. Each must gain an understanding of the other's capabilities and expertise. Communication helps to bridge gaps and aids new knowledge gained from research to be commercialized (the process of innovation).

Finally, it was realized that tools are needed to advance the frontiers in every field. These tools, as identified by workshop participants, come in the form of (1) infrastructure, (2) intellectual property, and (3) metrics, evaluation, and assessment.[1]

---

[1]Process measures should be developed keeping NSF internal reporting requirements in mind.

Table F.1

Summary of Key Workshop Findings and Recommendations

Background/ Summary	Concerns	Process/How to Make It Happen	Recommendations for PFI	Recommendations for NSF
People: Workforce				
One estimate is that by 2015, possibly 2010, the United States will not have enough skilled workers. The United States needs to involve *all* of its citizens, including those who are not traditionally involved in innovation currently ("recruit and retain").

The needs and differences (cultural, age, skill, motivational) among students must be analyzed. A one-size-fits-all type program in the educational system does not work. Workers today will have to do lifelong learning to stay fully functional in a | Determine how to keep/retain students in the same state in which they grew up (especially EPSCoR states).

Determine how to reach all stakeholders, especially minority-owned businesses.

Money from other federal sources (e.g., national labs) does not count toward matching funds when it should.

K-12 programs do not fully address the science, technology, engineering, and math problems in the United States. | Buy-in from all stakeholders: faculty, students.

Communication systems that people can access and use.

Buy-out time for those involved in mentoring, scheduling, coordinating, or sabbaticals.

Internships in which members of the private sector work for a university (instead of always being the other way).

A workforce-training program with a complementary placement program.

Student entrepreneur training.

Identification of talent at early age. | Include a K-12 aspect or some type of mentoring program to PFI grants.

Include funding in each PFI grant to pay for a coordinator of activities between the partners.

Prolong the PFI program for long period of time, like EPSCoR.

Pay for more of the industry participation, especially small businesses. | Leverage more with private foundations while developing a more formal, strategic approach to sustain funding.

Have international consultants to learn global best practices in workforce development.

Establish small business development center-like program for engineering.

Consider broader applicant pool for any RFPs (e.g., foundations, school districts).

Establish clearinghouse (searchable database) of programs funded by NSF.

Be more aggressive: Leverage with the Department of Education to have a stronger voice for the K-12 community (K-12 science, technology, engineering, and mathematics program—STEM).

In grants involving K-12, increase emphasis on state and national standards. |

Table F.1 (continued)

Background/ Summary	Concerns	Process/How to Make It Happen	Recommendations for PFI	Recommendations for NSF
technologically innovative society. Workers must be given the means to continue education, through both the educational system and support from employers.				Target education and training for specific grants. Leverage existing programs to bridge problems using multi-agency collaboration. Create unique facilities for education and training for future workforce. Use an integrated systems approach to education, to consider K-12 all the way to Ph.D. level. Create partnership between universities, the private sector, and state/regional government. Allow flexibility for those who either want to take time out of regular job to train/educate workforce or to get additional training. Create a job placement program for those who go through workforce training.
People: Partners				
The success of partnerships depends on the individuals involved. Those persons must be driven and	Differences in objectives of partners could hinder the achievement of goals.	For a start-up, need a charismatic and convincing inventor or PI—a passionate and visionary leader.		Ensure equality among partners. Be involved in matchmaking of partners. Enable partnerships. Promote "PFI" mentality.

Table F.1 (continued)

Background/ Summary	Concerns	Process/How to Make It Happen	Recommendations for PFI	Recommendations for NSF
committed and have well-defined roles and responsibilities.	The university partner wants to publicize research right away, industry partner wants to keep findings confidential. A balance is needed. Passionate leaders are rare and expensive. Lack of communication, understanding, and information flows between partners. Culture clash—difference in perspectives between the academic, industrial, and legal communities.	A change in the culture; promotion of diversity. Identification of strategic partners. A network of people with shared interests, alumni, etc. A win-win situation for both partners to cement commitment toward the effort. Clearly defined priorities, which can be communicated during negotiations (honest expression of goals and agendas). Alignment of expectations (returns, confidentiality, and timing). Identification of comparative advantage (strengths and weaknesses). Definition of goals, customers, products/services, and competitors—creation of a business plan.		

Table F.1 (continued)

Background/ Summary	Concerns	Process/How to Make It Happen	Recommendations for PFI	Recommendations for NSF
		Definition of and measurement of outcomes, benchmarks, and assets. Communication and mutual understanding among all involved.		
Ideas: Communication				
A dialogue between and among university and industry is essential to (1) find potential partners and (2) learn new information/new knowledge. The three Cs should be followed: communicate, coordinate, and collaborate.	Determine how to promote and enable communication between the academic sector and the private sector. Deal with any lack of information flows. Determine how other people can learn what ideas are available. Decide how to interact with the people who do have ideas.	Websites such as mainscience.org, which includes proposals and abstracts for researchers to search. Videos and CD ROMs. Knowledge management system to track what the university is doing in research and in education (search engine for industry to use). Networking small and large businesses, university, and government (collaborations, clusters). Community review of ideas (with technical facilitator in charge).	PFI is a good way to bring industry and university together. The program should grow larger to ensure that more opportunities are available.	Continue having more forums such as this workshop to bring people together, but ensure 50–50 participation by university and industry.

Table F.1 (continued)

Background/ Summary	Concerns	Process/How to Make It Happen	Recommendations for PFI	Recommendations for NSF
		Visibility of ideas. Dissemination of ideas, information, and publications. Good university-industry relations office. Professional and technical societies. Proactive approaches. Outreach. Communication of ideas and implementation of plans both vertically (within organization) and horizontally (across organizations). Education of stakeholders about communicating early on the ideas and research that may be of interest to them and others. Good market practices.		
		Ideas: Commercialization		
Commercially useful research has many characteristics, such as a potentially high pay-off, potential end user	It is great that industry can commercialize university research. However, this should not distract the university from	Education of end users, the consumers. Establishment of IP policies with differences between academic and	Partners should be equal; university should not be the prime contractor.	Enable partnerships. Be a matchmaker for potential partnerships between university and industry.

Table F.1 (continued)

Background/ Summary	Concerns	Process/How to Make It Happen	Recommendations for PFI	Recommendations for NSF
consumer interest, broad commercial benefits, and proprietary advantage over state of the art. Yet, the process of moving an idea from the research phase to the commercialization phase can be difficult.	its main mission of creating both new knowledge and workers.　Timelines are different between university and industry. University takes a period of time to complete research. Industry wants a solution in a very short timeframe.　Most faculty reward structures are based on the number of publications. They should be restructured to also reward those that develop new products or spin-off companies. There is a lack of capital.	private sectors' policies realized. Access to venture capital. A business plan created at the beginning.		Maintain a web page that academics can use throughout their academic career to advertise their skills, to be accessed by industry.　Create more programs, such as PFI, that encourage university to engage with industry to obtain funds.　Fund research to develop industry and businesses.　Encourage universities to support SBIR program. This will provide another means for university scientists to commercialize their research.

Tools: Infrastructure

Background/ Summary	Concerns	Process/How to Make It Happen	Recommendations for PFI	Recommendations for NSF
The basic foundation for research is the infrastructure. A single tool is not effective; a combination of tools is needed (some that may be obtained through		Incubators/accelerators. Funds/leveraging. Facilities (labs, equipment, and communications). Best practices (including standard operating procedures).		Integrate the economic development field with the university technology field.　The EPSCoR program is better promoted and more integrated into the economic development structure.

Table F.1 (continued)

Background/ Summary	Concerns	Process/How to Make It Happen	Recommendations for PFI	Recommendations for NSF
partnering) to build this foundation.		Use of the Internet (and Internet 2). Educated faculty. Business services.		Disseminate information. Support development of modal programs. Assist in grant preparation to lead to greater infrastructure development. Do *not* turn into economic development agency. Act as a catalyst (e.g., for other agencies). Fund diverse group of institutions. Continue PFI program, and others such as Integrative Graduate Education and Research Traineeship, GOALI, and REU. Create a program similar to REU for entrepreneurs and entrepreneurial experience for undergraduates.
Tools: Intellectual Property				
Three important questions to think about with IP are: (1) Who is the assignee on the patent?	There may be unmet expectations from agreements (ownership, control, and benefits).	Agreement, business process, partners, and marketing to effectively use patents.		Generate structures to promote the needed communication regarding IP. Expand industrial participation in forums (e.g., workshops).

Table F.1 (continued)

Background/ Summary	Concerns	Process/How to Make It Happen	Recommendations for PFI	Recommendations for NSF
(2) Who has the right to commercialize, sell, or otherwise use the IP? (3) Who gets to share in the profits from the use of the IP? There is a major difference between IP from industry-funded research and federally funded research (i.e., Bayh-Dole Act). Profit to universities from IP is not strictly in a monetary form. Profits/rewards involve revenues from licensing and patents, sponsored research, student internships, funding for equipment, patents counting as a publication, opportunities for consulting, and promotion and tenure.	There could be a lack of awareness of issues on both sides of the partnership. Lack of awareness of the different needs of small and large businesses could be a hindrance. As the number of collaborators increases (each with different IP policies), complications occur. Difficulty in contracts and negotiations could arise—both university and industry have to realize that each is a partner not a sole owner.	Settlement of IP and patent issues a long time before reaching innovation research centers. Improvement in patent cycle. Training programs in IP issues for faculty. An office with competent, well-trained staff and a "brokerage service" that brings together VCs and faculty with patents. Use of the Internet to find the different kinds of patents already available (Patent and Trademark Office website).		Use best practices and lessons learned in IP. Give more support to those schools with small IP portfolios.

Table F.1 (continued)

Background/Summary	Concerns	Process/How to Make It Happen	Recommendations for PFI	Recommendations for NSF
		Tools: Metrics, Evaluation, and Assessment		
Records should be kept from the start. A process should be developed to collect information that could be useful to those in charge of the program. It is important to understand what happened with both winners and losers. Through failures, bottlenecks can be identified and removed for the future.	Self-evaluation is difficult to do without some bias. What would have happened anyway, the counterfactual?	Process Measures Are meetings held regularly? Are things produced that can be disseminated? LISTSERVES? Websites? What is leadership structure organization? How was the partnership formed? How will the venture be expanded? Are there specific goals to be achieved? Were they achieved? Integration of personnel and infrastructure—how much is really shared in a partnership? Outcome Measures How many patents were applied for? How many patents were awarded? What are the demographics?	PFI offers short-term nonrenewable grants (2–3 years). Better to measure the process than overall success or failure of program. Since grants are given in a wide range of subjects, it is more effective to see what works and what does not.	Evaluate selection criteria. Evaluate quality of technical assistance provided. Evaluate grant-making criteria. Determine timeliness of award. Reward success—provide phase II funding for firms that are successful in the partnership. Work with PIs to develop metrics.

Table F.1 (continued)

Background/ Summary	Concerns	Process/How to Make It Happen	Recommendations for PFI	Recommendations for NSF
		Is it a self-perpetuating project? Will future partnerships be developed? Has capacity been built as a result of the process? Did the partnership survive, although the innovation failed? And vice versa? How was the quality of the work? How long was the partnership sustained after the funding ended? What was the value added to the personnel?		Enhance communication and cross-talk among partners for lessons learned, best practices. Rotate regional conferences of PIs.
		Sustainability		
A large investment in resources such as capital, infrastructure, people, time, and energy makes sustainability a pertinent issue. For that type of effort, a plan that will ensure the continuation and livelihood of a partnership should be developed.	Is the partnership genuine, or is it a marriage of convenience? A marriage of convenience is mainly concerned about money. A genuine partnership wants to grow, build, and sustain itself. Lack of funding for operational support, PR,	Keep a mixed model of investment (internal resources, including skunk works; grant funding, philanthropy; private sector—angels, VC, corporate). Find committed customer(s). Character of innovation matters. Incremental improvements can ensure future.	Proposal should include plans for sustainability.	

Table F.1 (continued)

Background/ Summary	Concerns	Process/How to Make It Happen	Recommendations for PFI	Recommendations for NSF
	and a visionary leader could hamper efforts.	Keep goals flexible. Mobilize intellectual and economic resources residing in a region to realize the opportunity in key emerging technology sectors to build a sustainable regional economy. Have competitors as collaborators (co-opetition). Use public relations to attract potential funders who will help sustain efforts. Document success. "Sell" previous success.		

OBSERVATIONS ON PFI EVALUATION CRITERIA

In light of the NSF's commitment to measuring performance and results, there was strong support for undertaking a proper evaluation of the PFI program. The preceding chapters reported on a number of specific outcome measures and process measures (signposts) that were suggested to assess program performance; we now turn to some of the broader principles that were articulated (or could be inferred) from the workshop discussions.

SOME GENERAL PRINCIPLES FOR EVALUATION

Underlying beliefs about the fundamental nature of the innovation process and the characteristics of successful partnerships importantly shaped views regarding appropriate selection and assessment criteria for innovative partnerships and the sorts of foundations that are necessary to ensure their sustainability. Participants posited a number of general principles that might guide the development of evaluation criteria for the PFI program:

- It is important to measure both innovation and partnerships.

- There are important differences between *program* evaluation criteria, i.e., criteria by which the benefits and costs of the overall PFI program should be judged, and *project* evaluation criteria that are needed to generate data for the overall program assessment. Program evaluation criteria should be established before project evaluation criteria and should explicitly tie project-level measures to the larger program evaluation.

- There are important differences between *outcome* measures that would be measurable only at the end of a partnership and *process* measures that could be used while the project was under way.[1] Outcome measures should be established before process measures.

- In all cases, participants favored the development of "objective" measures of evaluation, recognizing the difficulties in developing such measures.

- Benchmarking and establishing indicators as a standard of comparison need to be done at the beginning of a project to establish a continuous data flow and ensure that relevant data are not lost.

- Finally, workshop discussants asked who (e.g., the PIs themselves or independent evaluators) should perform the outcome evaluations and when? Although it is important that PIs provide input on the performance measures that will be used, most supported independent, paid evaluators.

OUTCOME MEASURES

There was some agreement on the principles that should guide the development of metrics, even if there remained a number of unresolved questions:

- Many favored development of a "strong logic" for the choice of goals and metrics to assess their accomplishment, while providing the flexibility necessary to enable application to a wide range of projects.[2]

- The PFI program's multiple program goals has led to diversity in the PFI portfolio of projects, which also promotes multiple project goals and makes it difficult to make comparisons. Although discussants agreed that not every project needed to fulfill each

---

[1]For example, outcome measures were viewed as end results and summative in nature, useful for assessing goal accomplishment at the end of a partnership, whereas process measures were seen as real-time and formative, useful for providing feedback for improving the program.

[2]The metrics used should depend on the goals and the emphasis of work (e.g., workforce vs. technical studies).

PFI goal, and that projects should be evaluated on the basis of what they originally proposed to do, questions remained as to whether multiple goals should be equally weighted in an evaluation.

- Benchmarks need to be established, even if those benchmarks are somewhat imperfect. Initially, one may be able only to establish benchmarks derived from the goals of the partnership and then to ask whether (or the degree to which) it achieved specific goals; these may change over time, but this provides an initial basis for comparison, or straw man.[3]

- Some respondents argued that it was more important to get answers to fundamental questions rather than more esoteric ones that might need to rely on sophisticated measurement techniques. For example, how was the partnership formed? How was the venture expanded? What were the specific goals to be achieved? Were the goals achieved?

In navigating these various imperatives and challenges, workshop discussions suggested a combination of top-down and bottom-up approaches that would need to be connected to perform both program- and project-level outcome assessments:

- On the one hand, participants supported a top-down approach in which program evaluation criteria first were established based upon program goals, and project-level outcomes mapped to these larger program goals;

- On the other hand, it was clear that judgments about the outcome of the overall PFI program rested upon a summation of judgments about the individual projects, and the heterogeneity of the projects suggested that a fair amount of tailoring might be required.

To illuminate some of these interdependencies, we now summarize views regarding the top-down program-level outcome measures that

---

[3]For example, a partnership might have the goal of funding 12 graduate students, with seven of them going to work in this area after graduation and the project self-sustaining in three years. At the end of the evaluation period, the partnership might have fallen short of its goals, but the initial goals would provide a seemingly reasonable initial point of comparison.

derive from PFI program goals and the sorts of summative judgments that will need to be made. We then discuss workshop participants' views on project-level outcome measures and how these project-level measures might be summed in such a way that they can be reconnected to the program-level evaluation.

Program-Level Outcome Measures

Workshop participants argued that the PFI program should largely be evaluated on the basis of whether it achieved its goals, including stimulating the transformation of knowledge, sustaining innovation, and transferring technology; training and workforce development; catalyzing economic development of states and regions; and broadening participation in the innovation enterprise.

Leaving aside the inherent difficulties of developing outcome measures for these goals,[4] there also was some support for evaluating the program on the basis of several less easily measured outcomes. Among these were estimating the value added by the partnership, including the types of benefits, number of beneficiaries, and distribution of these benefits; the spread of ideas on how to partner effectively and ensure best practices; the sustainability and long-term effect of the partnerships; the amount of new knowledge gained; and whether the award increased the propensity of awardees to partner more in the future.

There also was some support for the notion that the outcome measures should be capable of informing decisions about how to improve the PFI program: to learn which things are working, identify bottlenecks and "failure nuggets" and remove them, and how to better perform risk analyses. There also was a strong sentiment that such evaluative information could facilitate the identification of what the most effective strategies might be and what might constitute best practices at the national level.

---

[4]One challenge in evaluating outcomes is the inherent difficulty of counterfactual analyses. For the PFI program, one needs to establish that the partnership would not have occurred and the stream of benefits that resulted from the partnership would not have been seen had the PFI grant not been provided. To do this, one would have to interview the proposers of those projects that were not funded and discover whether those partnerships were in fact established even without PFI funding.

Project-Level Outcome Measures

Although workshop participants felt that project evaluation metrics should be tied to the PFI program's stated goals, they also recognized that the partnerships were of many different types, promoting different mixes of the program goals. The key issues regarding outcome evaluations at the project level, then, were determining which goals applied to which project and what combination of metrics accordingly should be used to evaluate goal accomplishment for each, so that these results could provide the data necessary for the program assessment.

Additionally, some expressed the view that at the project level, projects could (and should) be evaluated largely on the basis of whether they had met the specific goals detailed in the original proposal to the PFI. To this end, it was believed that principal investigators should initiate conversations with the NSF over which criteria would be used to assess which outcomes of their partnership.[5]

PROCESS MEASURES

Program-Level Signposts

The program-level signposts were seen as summative, based upon project-level measures, described next.

Project-Level Signposts

As was described in preceding appendixes, attendees advocated project-level process measures (signposts) of two general kinds. The first kind focused on the progress of the partnership in achieving its innovation goals (which could indicate whether partnership activities were leading toward results); the second focused on the characteristics of the partnership that could indicate whether the partnership was using available instruments in pursuit of the correct actions.

---

[5]Although the idea may have some merit, there was no suggestion that PFI applicants should include in their application a suggested set of evaluation measures for their project.

EVALUATING THE NSF'S OWN SUPPORT

Finally, consistent with the view that the evaluation process pre-
sented the NSF with an opportunity to turn the lens on itself in an
effort to improve its support for innovation, attendees suggested that
the partnerships should be asked to evaluate the NSF's support during the PFI program and the extent to which that support helped
their partnership. It was unclear how best to acquire this information (e.g., by open-ended responses or a by standardized rating
scheme), but the basic aim was to elicit partners' views on such
questions as whether the program had been a success and worthwhile experiment from their vantage point, whether they would rec-
ommend the program to others, and what they learned about bootstrapping the innovation process. The project-level evaluations of
the value of the NSF's support also were viewed as summative and
easily aggregated for the program as a whole.

Some also saw program-level process measures as the place for the
NSF to turn the lens on itself regarding selection and grant-making
criteria, the quality of the technical assistance it provides, and other
issues.[6] The quality of the technical assistance provided by the NSF
can be summed from the individual project-level assessments of how
appropriate and helpful that technical assistance was.

Workshop participants identified a wide range of challenges related
to the methodology for evaluating individual projects and the program as a whole and in some cases offered practical suggestions regarding how best to implement an evaluation of the PFI program.
We now consolidate and summarize these observations and
suggestions.

- *The Difficulties of Evaluation in Observational Studies.* One
  challenge arises from the fact that a PFI evaluation would not be
  a controlled experiment[7] but an observational study, requiring

---

[6]For example, the time it takes to make an award was seen as important.

[7]In other words, projects were not randomly selected to receive a treatment (funding),
which would have enabled a comparison between those that were funded and those
that were not.

careful handling of potential bias.[8] To evaluate outcomes in such a setting, one needs to compare the outcomes of the chosen partnerships with some referent, but it was somewhat unclear exactly what that referent should be. Should a partnership's experience be compared to a counterfactual where the partnership did not receive PFI funding? What sort of confidence could one have in such a comparison? If partnerships are to be compared to projects whose proposals were not selected by the PFI program, how should the inherent biases be handled?

- *Self-Evaluation Versus Independent Evaluators.* There was support for including stakeholders in determining how their projects should be measured, but there was somewhat mixed support for the broader principle of self-evaluations. On the one hand, some considered the prospect of self-evaluation as presenting an opportunity that might be abused; others perceived a financial involvement that lent credence to self-evaluation and straightforward numbers that partners can provide. In light of the concern that self-reported measures could be biased, there was broad support for bringing in an external evaluator; the point also was made that NSF programs require a paid, outside evaluator for all projects.

- *Maintaining Records.* Another challenge was collecting and maintaining the necessary records to inform the evaluation; it is important that partners establish a process early in the project for collecting and maintaining records that can provide the NSF with relevant performance information. Some argued that incentives might be established, for example, tying the evaluation to the collection of information that also could be used later in marketing the project. For others, the main purpose was not so much to evaluate a particular project but to evaluate the overall program. This information was seen to be useful in coming to conclusions regarding what works and what does not and for supporting recommendations to policymakers so that program design can be improved.

---

[8]The selected partnerships were those that appeared to have the most promising proposals, and those that were not selected had proposals that were, in some sense, judged inferior.

- *Time Horizon for Evaluation.* Some thought that the time horizon of the PFI program was too short to be able to ascertain the program's effect on innovation and sustainability. For them, it was just too short a time scale for an evaluation. Some suggested a "3+2" year evaluation period—three years for the initial support, with two years of follow-up on outcomes. By the same token, a two-to-three-year time horizon was seen as probably being long enough to evaluate the NSF's role as a catalyst.

- *Data Reliability.* Several workshop participants expressed concern about the comprehensiveness, validity, and reliability of performance data.[9] Observing that data can be no more accurate than the way it is reported, it is important to make data collection as simple as possible. The observation was made that too many studies hide behind a great deal of complexity, and it is quite difficult to establish that the underlying data are even valid. Given that the PFI program is small, it should be relatively easy to interview all participants.

---

[9]They cited the case of the SBIR reauthorization as evidence of the importance of reliable and valid data.

BIBLIOGRAPHY

Alesina, Alberto, and Eliana Ferrara, "The Determinants of Trust," National Bureau of Economic Research, NBER Working Paper 7621, Cambridge, Massachusetts, March 2000.

American Council on Education, *Working Together, Creating Knowledge: The University-Industry Initiative,"* Item No. 309142, Washington, D.C., 2001.

BankBoston Economics Department, *MIT: The Impact of Innovation*, Boston, Massachusetts, 1997.

Behrens, Teresa R., and Denis O. Gray, "Unintended Consequences of Cooperative Research: Impact of Industry Sponsorship on Climate for Academic Freedom and Other Graduate Student Outcome," *Research Policy*, Vol. 30, 2001, pp. 179–199.

Bloom, Gordon F., "A Note on Hicks's Theory of Invention," *The American Economic Review*, Vol. 36, No. 1., March 1946, pp. 83–96.

Bordogna, Joseph, presentation at the National Science Foundation Partnerships for Innovation Planning Workshop, Arlington, Virginia, March 10, 2000.

Borrus, Michael, and Jay Stowsky, "Technology Policy and Economic Growth," in Lewis M. Branscomb and James H. Keller (eds.), *Investing in Innovation: Creating a Research and Innovation Policy That Works*, Harvard University Press, Cambridge, Massachusetts, 1998, pp. 40–63.

Branscomb, Lewis M., "From Science Policy to Research Policy," in Lewis M. Branscomb and James H. Keller (eds.), *Investing in Innovation: Creating a Research and Innovation Policy That Works*,

Harvard University Press, Cambridge, Massachusetts, 1998, pp. 112–142.

Carrincazeaux, Christophe, Yannick Lung, and Alain Rallet, "Proximity and Localisation of Corporate R&D Activities," *Research Policy*, Vol. 30, 2001, pp. 777–789.

Cozzens, Susan E., *Assessment of Fundamental Science Programs in the Context of the Government Performance and Results Act (GPRA)*, RAND, MR-707.0-OSTP, Santa Monica, California, October 1995.

David, Paul A., and Bronwyn H. Hall, "Heart of Darkness: Modeling Public-Private Funding Interactions Inside the R&D Black Box," *Research Policy*, Vol. 29, 2000, pp. 1165–1183.

De Graaf, Adriann M., "Government, University, and Industry Linkages," in National Research Council, Board on Science, Technology, and Economic Policy, *A Review of the Sandia Science and Technology Park Initiative*, National Academy Press, Washington, D.C., 1999, pp. 59–60.

Ember, Lois, "Encouraging Entrepreneurship: Caltech Facilitates High-Tech Start-Up Companies; Pasadena, Private Incubators Nurture Their Developments, *Chemical and Engineering News*, Vol. 78, No. 32, August 7, 2000, pp. 17–29.

Feller, Irwin, "Discussant," in National Research Council, Board on Science, Technology, and Economic Policy, *A Review of the Sandia Science and Technology Park Initiative*, National Academy Press, Washington, D.C., 1999, pp. 41–43.

Florida, Richard, "The Role of the University: Leveraging Talent, Not Technology," *Issues in Science and Technology*, Vol. XV, No. 4, Summer 1999, pp. 67–73.

Fox, Marye Anne, "A University Perspective on Partnerships," presentation at a National Science Foundation workshop, Partnerships: Building a New Foundation for Innovation, Arlington, Virginia, June 18–19, 2001.

Fountain, Jane E., "Social Capital: A Key Enabler of Innovation," in Lewis M. Branscomb and James H. Keller (eds.), *Investing in Inno-*

vation: Creating a Research and Innovation Policy That Works, Harvard University Press, Cambridge, Massachusetts, 1998, pp. 85–111.

Freeman, C., "Network of Innovators, A Synthesis of Research Issues," *Research Policy*, Vol. 20, No. 5, 1991, pp. 499–514.

Ganz-Brown, C., "Patent Policies to Fine Tune Commercialization of Government-Sponsored University Research," *Science and Public Policy*, Vol. 26, No. 6, December 1999.

Glaeser, Edward L., David Laibson, Jose A. Scheinkman, Christine L. Soutter, "What is Social Capital? The Determinants of Trust and Trustworthiness," National Bureau of Economic Research, NBER Working Paper 7216, Cambridge, Massachusetts, July 1999.

Good, Mary, "International View," presentation at a National Science Foundation workshop, Partnerships: Building a New Foundation for Innovation, Arlington, Virginia, June 18–19, 2001.

Government-University-Industry Research Roundtable, *Overcoming Barriers to Collaborative Research: Report of a Workshop*, National Academy Press, Washington, D.C., 1999.

Griliches, Zvi, "The Search for R&D Spillovers," NBER Working Paper 3768, Cambridge, Massachusetts, 1991.

Griliches, Zvi, "R&D and Productivity: Econometric Results and Measurement Issues," in Paul Stoneman (ed.), *Handbook of the Economics of Innovation & Technological Change*, Basil Blackwell Ltd., Oxford, 1995, pp. 52–89.

Guston, David H., "Technology Transfer and the Use of CRADAs at the National Institutes of Health," in Lewis M. Branscomb and James H. Keller (eds.), *Investing in Innovation: Creating a Research and Innovation Policy That Works*, Harvard University Press, Cambridge, Massachusetts, 1998, pp. 221–249.

Hanushek, Eric A., and Byung Nak Song, "The Dynamics of Postwar Industrial Location," *The Review of Economics and Statistics*, Vol. 60, No. 4, November 1978, pp. 515–522.

Henderson, R., A. Jaffe, and M. Trajtenberg, "Universities as a Source of Commercial Technology: A Detailed Analysis of University Patenting, 1965–88," *The Review of Economics and Statistics,* Vol. LXXX, No. 1, February 1998, pp. 119–127.

Hicks, Diana, Tony Breitzman, Dominic Olivastro, and Kimberly Hamilton, "The Changing Composition of Innovative Activity in the U.S.—A Portrait Based on Patent Analysis," *Policy Research,* Vol. 30, 2001, pp. 681–703.

Hill, Christopher T., "The Advanced Technology Program: Opportunities for Enhancement," in Lewis M. Branscomb and James H. Keller (eds.), *Investing in Innovation: Creating a Research and Innovation Policy That Works,* Harvard University Press, Cambridge, Massachusetts, 1998, pp. 144–173.

Hurt, John, "Overview of the Partnerships for Innovation Program," presentation at a National Science Foundation workshop, Partnerships: Building a New Foundation for Innovation, Arlington, Virginia, June 18–19, 2001.

Industrial Research Institute, Government-University-Industry Research Roundtable, and Council on Competitiveness, *Industry-University Research Collaborations: Report of a Workshop,* National Academy Press, Washington, D.C., 1996.

Jaffe, Adam B., "Measurement Issues," in Lewis M. Branscomb and James H. Keller (eds.), *Investing in Innovation: Creating a Research and Innovation Policy That Works,* Harvard University Press, Cambridge, Massachusetts, 1998, pp. 64–84.

Kaufmann, Alexander, and Franz Todtling, "Science-Industry Interaction in the Process of Innovation: The Importance of Boundary-Crossing Between Systems," *Research Policy,* Vol. 30, 2001, pp. 791–804.

Keller, Wolfgang, "The Geography and Channels of Diffusion at the World's Technology Frontier," National Bureau of Economic Research, NBER Working Paper 8150, Cambridge, Massachusetts, March 2001.

Kelley, Maryellen, "Lessons from the Advanced Technology Program," in National Research Council, Board on Science, Technology, and Economic Policy, *The Small Business Innovation Research Program: Challenges and Opportunities*, National Academy Press, Washington, D.C., 1999, pp. 93–95.

Love, James H., and Stephen Roper, "Location and Network Effects on Innovation Success: Evidence for UK, German and Irish Manufacturing Plants," *Research Policy*, Vol. 30, 2001, pp. 643–661.

Luger, Michael, "The Research Triangle Experience," in National Research Council, Board on Science, Technology, and Economic Policy, *A Review of the Sandia Science and Technology Park Initiative*, National Academy Press, Washington, D.C., 1999, pp. 35–38 and 92–101.

Luger, M. I., and H. A. Goldstein, *Technology in the Garden: Research Parks and Regional Economic Development*, University of North Carolina Press, Chapel Hill, North Carolina, 1991.

Malecki, Edward J., *Technology and Economic Development: The Dynamics of Local, Regional and National Competitiveness*, 2d Edition, Addison Wesley Longman, London, 1997.

Malecki, Edward J., "The Conditions for Success," National Research Council, Board on Science, Technology, and Economic Policy, *A Review of the Sandia Science and Technology Park Initiative*, National Academy Press, Washington, D.C., 1999, pp. 56–58.

Mansfield, Edwin, "Academic Research and Industrial Innovation," *Research Policy*, Vol. 20, No. 1, February 1991a, pp. 1–12.

Mansfield, Edwin, "Social Returns from R&D: Findings, Methods, and Limitations," *Research, Technology, and Management*, Vol. 34, No. 6, November-December 1991b, pp. 24–27.

Mazzoleni, R., and R. Nelson, "The Benefits and Costs of Strong Patent Protection: A Contribution to the Current Debate," *Research Policy*, Vol. 27, 1998, pp. 113–124.

Milbergs, Egils, "Industry Perspective on Partnerships," presentation at a National Science Foundation workshop, Partnerships: Building a New Foundation for Innovation, Arlington, Virginia, June 18–19, 2001, available at http://www.rand.org/scitech/stpi/Partnerships/milbergs.pdf.

Mowery, David C., "The Roles and Contributions of R&D Collaboration: Matching Policy Goals and Design," prepared for hearings of the National Science Policy Study, Committee on Science, U.S. House of Representatives, Washington, D.C., March 11, 1998.

Mowery, D., R. Nelson, B. Sampart, and A. Ziedonis. "The Growth of Patenting and Licensing by U.S. Universities: An Assessment of the Effects of the Bayh-Dole Act of 1980," *Research Policy*, in press.

National Research Council, Board on Science, Technology, and Economic Policy, *The Small Business Innovation Research Program: Challenges and Opportunities*, National Academy Press, Washington, D.C., 1999.

National Research Council, Board on Science, Technology, and Economic Policy, *A Review of the Sandia Science and Technology Park Initiative*, National Academy Press, Washington, D.C., 1999.

National Research Council, Committee on Visionary Manufacturing Challenges, Board on Manufacturing and Engineering Design, Commission on Engineering and Technical Systems, *Visionary Manufacturing Challenges for 2020*, National Academy Press, Washington, D.C., 1998.

National Science Board, "Total Expenditures for Industrial R&D (Financed by Company, Federal, and Other Funds), by Industry and Size of Company: 1985–97," *Science and Engineering Indicators 2000*, Washington, D.C., 2000.

National Science Foundation, *Retention of the Best Science and Engineering Graduates in Science and Engineering*, NSF 99-321, Washington, D.C., January 1999.

National Science Foundation, Office of Legislative and Public Affairs, "NSF Recommends Funding for 24 Partnerships to Foster Local Innovation," news release No. NSF PR-00-68, September 29, 2000.

National Science Foundation, *FY 2002 GPRA Performance Plan*, Washington, D.C., April 2001.

Norling, Parry, "Structuring and Managing R&D Work Processes— Why Bother?" *CHEMTECH*, October 1997, pp. 12–16.

O'Brien, Thomas, and Terry Fadem, "Identifying New Business Opportunities," *Research-Technology Management,* September-October 1999, pp. 15–19.

Popper, Steven W., *Economic Approaches to Measuring the Performance and Benefits of Fundamental Science,* RAND, MR-708.0-OSTP, Santa Monica, California, October 1995.

Popper, Steven W., Caroline S. Wagner, and Eric V. Larson, *New Forces at Work: Industry Views Critical Technologies,* RAND, MR-1008-OSTP, Santa Monica, California, 1998.

Popper, Steven W., and Caroline S. Wagner, *New Foundations for Growth: The U.S. Innovation System Today and Tomorrow; An Executive Summary,* RAND, MR-1338.0/1-OSTP, Santa Monica, California, January 2001.

Porter, Michael, *The Competitive Advantage of Nations,* Free Press, New York, 1990.

Roberts, Edward, and Charles Berry, "Entering New Businesses: Selecting Strategies for Success," *Sloan Management Review,* Spring 1985, pp. 3–17.

Salter, Ammon J., and Ben R. Martin, "The Economic Benefits of Publicly Funded Basic Research: A Critical Review," *Research Policy,* Vol. 30, 2001, pp. 509–532.

Saxenian, AnnaLee, *Regional Advantage: Culture and Competition in Silicon Valley and Route 128,* Harvard University Press, Cambridge, Massachusetts, 1996.

Schmandt, Jurgen, "The Austin Experience," in National Research Council, Board on Science, Technology, and Economic Policy, *A Review of the Sandia Science and Technology Park Initiative,* National Academy Press, Washington, D.C., 1999, pp. 39–40.

Shapira, Philip, "Manufacturing Extension: Performance, Challenges, and Policy Issues," in Lewis M. Branscomb and James H. Keller (eds.), *Investing in Innovation: Creating a Research and Innovation Policy That Works,* Harvard University Press, Cambridge, Massachusetts, 1998, pp. 250–275.

Stein, Jeremy C., "Waves of Creative Destruction: Firm-Specific Learning-by-Doing and the Dynamics of Innovation," *The Review of Economic Studies*, Vol. 64, No. 2, April 1997, pp. 265–288.

Sternberg, Rolf, "The Impact of Innovation Centres on Small Technology-Based Firms: The Example of the Federal Republic of Germany," *Small Business Economics*, Vol. 2, No. 2, 1990, pp. 105–118.

Stevens, Gregory, and John Burley, "3000 Raw Ideas = 1 Commercial Success," *Research-Technology Management*, Vol. 40, No. 3, May–June 1997, pp. 16–27.

Stokes, Donald, *Pasteur's Quadrant*, Brookings Institution Press, Washington, D.C., 1997.

Swann, G. M., M. Prevezer, and D. Stout, "The Dynamics of Industrial Clustering; International Comparisons in Computing and Biotechnology," Oxford University Press, Oxford, 1998.

Wallsten, Scott J., "The Effects of Government-Industry R&D Programs on Private R&D: The Case of the Small Business Innovation Research Program," *RAND Journal of Economics*, Vol. 31, No. 1, Spring 2000, pp. 82–100.

Wasserman, Ed, "Academic Entrepreneurs," *Chemical and Engineering News*, Vol. 78, No. 47, November 2000, p. 56.

"What Is the State of the New Economy," *Fast Company*, Issue 50, September 2001, p. 100.